EDITH STEIN
A BIOGRAPHY

K. Franke
Meerbüsch, Germany

Waltraud Herbstrith, O.C.D.

EDITH STEIN
A BIOGRAPHY

TRANSLATED BY
FATHER BERNARD BONOWITZ, O.C.S.O.

IGNATIUS PRESS   SAN FRANCISCO

Title of German original
Das Wahre Gesicht Edith Steins
© 1971 Verlagsgesellschaft Gerhard Kaffke mbH, Munich
Fifth edition
Published with ecclesiastical approval

First English edition
©1985 Harper and Row, New York

Cover design by Riz Boncan Marsella
Photographs from the Edith Stein Carmel

Second English edition
1992 Ignatius Press, San Francisco
ISBN 0–89870–410–3
Library of Congress catalogue number 92–71938
Printed in the United States of America

Contents

Foreword

August 9, 1982, marked the fortieth anniversary of the death of Edith Stein. On that day the great Jewish philosopher was honored on radio and television broadcasts, in books, periodicals, and newspapers, and by religious memorial services. The German Postal Service issued a commemorative stamp of her in January 1983, showing her dressed in her Carmelite habit. Throughout Germany she has come to be acknowledged as a model and inspiration; today there are schools, institutes, libraries, community centers, student residences, streets, and public squares all bearing her name.

> Edith Stein is one of the most significant women Germany has produced this century. All over the world, men and women of every profession and religious persuasion have recognized in her life—as a Jew, Christian, scholar, professional woman, and, finally, as a victim of totalitarianism—the marks of a follower of Jesus. Her goal was to assist in the formation of men and women conscious of their calling to live as committed Christians. Through her efforts in the area of equal rights, she hoped to lead women in particular to a sharper awareness of their specific mission within society and within the Church.[1]

During the January 14, 1983, *ad limina* visit[2] of the bishops of the southwest German region, Bishop Georg Moser brought up Edith Stein's name in his meeting with John Paul II. The Pope proved himself well informed about her life and

---

[1] "Sondermarke Edith Stein", in *Deutsche Tagespost,* no. 9, January 1983, pp. 6, 21–22.

[2] This is the regular visit of the bishops with the Pope in Rome.—TRANS.

martyrdom, and he expressed great pleasure that a Carmelite convent named after her had been established in Bishop Moser's own diocese.

Such widespread interest has resulted in the publication of a fifth, newly revised and expanded edition of *Edith Stein: A Biography*. A bibliography that attempts to give a representative overview of the current research and literature about Edith Stein has been appended. It does not, however, claim to be exhaustive.

I would like to express my thanks to Dr. Jan Nota, S.J., for enriching this biography with his introduction based on personal recollections of Edith Stein. My thanks are also due to my sister Carmelites Celine Mansutti and Gabrielle Dick for their work in reading and preparing the manuscript. I also wish to thank Dr. F. G. Friedmann (Munich) and Frau Wolfert-Herold (Freiburg) for their valuable suggestions and corrections.

Waltraud Herbstrith
Edith Stein Carmel, Tübingen
April 15, 1983

Introduction

It is a pleasure for me to write an introduction to the fifth edition of *Edith Stein*. I met Edith Stein in Echt, Holland, in November 1941, where I came to know her as a person who had continued to be a great philosopher after having become a Carmelite nun. It was in fact philosophy, so much a part of her very being, that provided the basis for our first encounter.

Since the end of 1938, Edith Stein had been living in the Carmel at Echt, forced to abandon her convent in Cologne after the anti-Semitic violence of the *Kristallnacht*.[1] The Dutch Jesuits had also moved recently to Valkenberg, since, as a result of the 1940 occupation of Holland, the Jesuit house in Maastricht had been commandeered by the Nazis. I myself was one of the young Dutch Jesuits who was living in Valkenberg. I had just finished working on my dissertation on Max Scheler. Though Edith Stein's own philosophical study, *Finite and Eternal Being* (called the "biography of her life" by Professors Alexander Koyré and Alois Dempf), had been set for publication by Borgmyer back in 1936, anti-Jewish laws in Germany had prevented its completion, and eventually the plates had been destroyed. Now the superiors at Echt decided to consult the Valkenberg Jesuits about the feasibility of having the work published either in Holland or Belgium. They also asked if a priest would be available to collaborate with Edith Stein. Father Hirschmann, a notable figure in German Catholicism, especially after Vatican II, was also in Valkenberg during the 1940s, and he recommended me to the

[1] The S.S. attack of November 8 and 9, 1938, was so called because of all the glass windows smashed in the synagogues. — TRANS.

Carmel at Echt. Such was the beginning of the brief but profound friendship that developed between Edith Stein and myself.

Despite her superiors' eagerness to see *Finite and Eternal Being* in print, Edith Stein herself was more realistic about the matter. She knew that in occupied Holland there was no chance of publication for a book by a Jewish author. During one conversation she told me, "I think it will have to be a posthumous work." These words, spoken without the least trace of bitterness, sounded tranquil, almost joyful. They gave me the feeling that Edith Stein refused to allow herself any illusions about the political situation. Instead, she insisted on preparing for the worst.

Edith Stein's concern for the truth extended beyond its application to herself to a concern for the truth *in se*. Not only did she want to hear the truth, even when it was at her own expense, she also had the courage to say it to and about others. Only by exaggeration could one claim that she never said anything negative about a person in his absence. I remember, for instance, how, for all her admiration for Heidegger's work, she couldn't stomach the self-serving attitude he and others had adopted toward Edmund Husserl during the Hitler era. As she wrote to Professor Vierneisel:

> Has there been any mention of Husserl's death in the Berlin newspapers? A copy of the obituary in the "Hamburger Fremdenblatt" came today—brief and terribly cold. Nothing of that kind can hurt our beloved master any more. He was already freed from everything earthly at the time of his death. But for posterity, you could almost apply Goethe's epigram[2] on those who misjudged Hans Sachs.[3]

----

[2] In one of his poems, Goethe consigns to a frog-pond those who have misjudged their master.—TRANS.

[3] Edith Stein, *Selbstbildnis in Briefen* II. Teil 1934–1942, Edith Steins Werke, Bd. IX (Druten: De Maas und Waler/Freiburg-Basel-Vienna: Herder, 1977), Letter 260, p. 103.

In his final years, German public opinion had turned against Husserl on account of his Jewish ancestry.

While I myself found her ability to recognize weaknesses in herself and others without condemning them to be a personally attractive trait, it was not a universally appreciated one. The same holds true for her deep sense of Jewishness and her love and commitment to Judaism; these did not always find a favorable reception in her Christian environment. Edith Stein told me that, even as an adolescent, she had refused to be governed by prevailing notions. Despite what she had been taught about the proper social roles of men and women, all that had mattered to her was the quest for truth—which, as far as she could see, was equally imposed on both sexes.

The fascinating thing to me about Edith Stein was that truth did not exist as an abstraction for her but as something incarnated in persons and therefore as inconceivable apart from love. Adrienne von Speyr was correct when she described Edith Stein's life as a convert as "service to the Church". For her, there could be no separation between Christ and his body—or Christ and his people. The Christ she had encountered as a phenomenologist was the one who had revealed himself within his Church, not some rationalistic projection of him. In the same way, Christ was a Jew, and Edith Stein felt proud to belong to his people.

Prior to 1933, Edith Stein was one of the few who recognized the catastrophe threatening the Jewish people. Unfortunately, her 1933 request to Pope Pius XI for an encyclical in defense of the Jews was not complied with at the time—due in large part to faulty handling of the matter. Nonetheless, it is heartening to know that shortly thereafter the Pope commissioned two Jesuits, Fathers La Farge and Grundlach, to compose a document condemning racial persecution. Though the outbreak of World War II and the death of the Pope prevented the publication of their efforts, parts of their work later appeared in speeches of Pius XII.[4]

---

[4] Jan H. Nota, S.J., "Edith Stein und der Entwurf für eine Enzyklika

Edith Stein's wish to offer her life for world peace and the preservation of her people should not, in my opinion, be taken as a manifestation of something unhealthy. Sacrifice for its own sake did not interest her; the active yearning for suffering and the retreat into subhuman passivity were both equally foreign. Years earlier she had compared the study of philosophy to a walk along the edge of an abyss. Now in Carmel, once again "on the brink", she had discovered in Christ the meaning of human existence and suffering. What she found drew her to surrender herself to God in union with him. Edith Stein was one of those Christians who lived out of a hope transcending optimism and pessimism. At one and the same time she could enthusiastically consider the idea of emigrating to the Carmel in Bethlehem and peacefully accept the likelihood of the project's failure.

I saw Edith Stein for the last time on July 16, 1942. That is the day the Carmelite Order celebrates as its patronal feast, "Our Lady of Mount Carmel", in commemoration of the first Carmelite friars who, back in the thirteenth century, established their life of prayer in the mountains near Haifa. When I arrived at the convent, Edith Stein asked me to deliver a homily at the Holy Hour. I felt a little nervous, having never preached in public since my ordination, but Edith Stein directed me to some beautiful Scripture texts found in the Carmelite Office and helped me to put the sermon together. In fact, she almost wrote it herself. Yet she did it all in a friendly, unassuming way, happy to have me take her suggestions. It occurred to me that Edith Stein's intellectual talents had in no way impaired the feminine side of her personality. She was anxious that I take back enough food for the return journey. She loved to show me photos of her family, and of Husserl and

gegen Rassismus und Atheismus", *Freiburger Rundbrief, Beiträge zur christlich-jüdischen Begegnung,* XXVI, no. 97/100 (Folge, 1974). This article also appeared in *Internationale Katholische Zeitschrift Kommunio* 5 (Cologne, 1976), pp. 154–66.

Scheler too. (Prior to his untimely death in 1928, Scheler, out of the appreciation and respect he felt for Edith Stein as a fellow philosopher, had referred to her phenomenological research a number of times in his final Cologne lectures on the theme of empathy. He had likewise frequently cited her work in his book *The Nature and Forms of Sympathy*.)

When I said goodbye to Edith Stein that July day, I had no idea it was the last time I would ever be able to do anything for her. For a while, I blamed myself for not having somehow tried to speed up the emigration process to Switzerland. Now, in retrospect, I don't think there actually was anything I could have done. We were all simply living from day to day. It was Edith Stein who understood better than the rest of us the full implications of the Nazi extermination policy. Only ten days after my visit to Echt, the Catholic bishops' letter of protest against the persecution of the Jews was publicly read in all the churches. On August 2, 1942, in retaliation for the Church's action, the S.S. arrested Edith Stein, along with many other Catholic Jews.

Edith Stein's obedience to her conscience led her to travel on unaccustomed paths. If the Jewish people seem to stand alone again today, her life and martyrdom are clear testimony that God's election of her people is an enduring one. She was a woman who gave herself fully to this world, yet always remembered that she and her fellow human beings were on their way to God. She was a scholar of considerable philosophical output and a superb translator, who always remained a person of such great reserve and humility that, despite her accomplishments, most people never suspected the measure of her greatness. And yet, when it comes to philosophy and religion, what else but humility is the basic condition for the discovery of truth?

On August 9, 1982, the fortieth anniversary of Edith Stein's death, I celebrated a memorial Mass in Tübingen along with the sisters of the Edith Stein Carmel. During that trip, I also had the opportunity to share my recollections at a number of liturgies held at Saint Johannes, the Tübingen parish church. On each of these occasions, I applied to Edith Stein the words inscribed at the Yad Vashem Memorial in Jerusalem in memory of the six million slaughtered Jews: "The mystery of redemption lies in remembrance."

I had visited Yad Vashem back in 1977, during a trimester as guest lecturer in Jerusalem. The trip affected me deeply. It is a place off the beaten track for most pilgrims and tourists. Every morning at eleven a memorial service is conducted for the victims of National Socialism. An impressive mosaic in a dimly lit hall carries the names and symbols of the twenty-two concentration camps: Auschwitz, Bergen-Belsen, Dachau, Mauthausen, . . . and so on. In front of an urn, filled with ashes of the martyrs, an eternal light is kept burning: "The mystery of redemption lies in remembrance." Hence the hall's other title, "Hall of Remembrance". We too should remember that Edith Stein is only one of six million Jews who were brutally exterminated. Let us be constantly vigilant to prevent such terrifying aberrations from ever threatening the nations of the world again.

Today, in Canada and the United States, interest in Edith Stein's personal witness and intellectual achievement is growing. At lectures and symposia, I frequently find myself asked to speak about some aspect of her life and work.

One of the most moving parts of the Mass I celebrated in Carmel on August 9, 1982, was the privilege I had afterward of speaking with others who had known Edith Stein personally. Three of her former students from Speyer were there, all of them teachers, as well as one of her colleagues—the painter Baroness Uta von Bodman, who, like Edith Stein, had lived for years with the community of Dominican sisters in Speyer. The four of them described her as a woman of deep culture and profound moral refinement. They remembered her as a teacher who had never needed to resort to discipline to control her classes.

Baroness von Bodman recalled that Edith Stein was not among those who had rejoiced at the German takeover of the Rhineland in the 1930s. "First there will be a persecution of the Jews in Germany," she had predicted, "but afterward the Church will have to suffer persecution too." The baroness also mentioned Edith Stein's insistence on the God-given equality of all people and her refusal to acknowledge any distinction of caste or class.[5]

It is my hope that new editions of Edith Stein's writings will make her thought accessible to a wider audience, both among students and among the general public. Only an in-depth study of her life and work can enable us to appreciate her understanding of human existence and help us to live out that existence ourselves, meaningfully and fraternally, in the midst of a troubled world.

> *Jan H. Nota, S.J.*
> *Professor of Philosophy and Phenomenology*
> *McMaster University, Hamilton, Ontario, Canada*

---

[5] Waltraud Herbstrith, "Zum 40. Todestag Edith Steins", in *Treffpunkt, Kontaktblatt des Teresianischen Karmel in Deutschland,* 12. Jg., no. 5 (October 1982), pp. 135–38.

Preface to the Fourth Edition

Dr. Erna Biberstein, Edith Stein's sister who died in America in January 1978, had the following to say about the present work:

> I still consider this to be one of the finest biographies there is of my sister. In addition to providing an affectionate account of her life, it offers a perceptive treatment of her inner development both as a philosopher and as a convert to Catholicism. Philosophically, the author demonstrates a thorough knowledge of phenomenology. Moreover, as a Carmelite, Sister Theresia[1] is also able to trace with expertise the spiritual aspect of Edith's maturation, particularly during her years in the convent. Despite the fact that she never knew Edith personally, she has managed in my opinion to produce a very true-to-life portrait of her.

Edith Stein's life, and the response it has generated among people of various age-groups, ought to encourage us. It began with a search for truth, justice, and peace that brought her in touch with people of widely differing outlooks. Exposure to Christianity, growing out of a number of close personal friendships with Christians, led to an experience of Christ's Cross and Resurrection years before her conversion. Yet rather than resulting in immediate membership in a Christian denomination, this encounter initiated a long process of internal reflection within the philosopher. During this time, she came to recognize with increasing clarity that thinking and knowing alone provided inadequate solutions to the fundamental problems of the individual and that only love, with its demand for surrender to another, was able to point to the discovery of self.

---

[1] This is the author's name in religious life. — TRANS.

For this is how Edith Stein functioned — as an honest and exacting thinker, diligent in opening up ways to the truth and yet gratefully accepting its manifestations as unexpected gifts. Tragic and incomprehensible as her decisions often seemed to outsiders and to her own Jewish family, they were always made only after long and serious deliberation. Already at the age of thirteen she had begun to make the internal break with her family by consciously abandoning the practice of prayer. That early atheistic stance was weakened in her university years through friendships with Christians; and eventually in 1922, to the surprise of many of her friends, the young disciple of Husserl was baptized. Though she chose initially to leave serious scholarship behind in order to take on a job teaching German with the Dominican sisters in Speyer, a few years afterward the Jesuit Erich Przywara restored her interest in academic research, and along with it her active orientation to the world and her fellow human beings, this time within the context of faith. From 1927 on, she began receiving numerous invitations from Germany, Switzerland, and Austria to speak on the subject of women's education and professional formation.

In 1932, Edith Stein obtained an appointment as lecturer at the German Institute for Educational Theory in Münster. Due to the "Aryan Laws", she lost her position after a single year of productive work, like so many others of Jewish descent. This, however, allowed her to fulfill her longstanding desire to enter religious life as a Carmelite nun. For five years she lived as a sister in the convent in Cologne; then, in the wake of the *Kristallnacht* of 1938, she fled to Holland and the Carmel in Echt. When the Nazi takeover of 1940 exposed her to the threat of anti-Semitic persecution once again, she realized with clear-headed intuition that the ultimate sacrifice was going to be required. She responded by asking God to accept her life as an offering for peace in the world, expressing her desire in three prayers of surrender and a final testament.

Edith Stein's premonitions were justified. For a long time, she had identified herself with the Old Testament figure of

Esther. Now it was her turn to plead before God for her people's deliverance and safety. "Lord God our King, God of Abraham, spare your people. They look upon us with hatred and seek to destroy us. They plan to make an end of us, your heritage from of old. Hear my pleading; have mercy on your inheritance. Turn our sorrow into joy, O Lord, that we may live to praise your name" (Esther 4:17ff.).

But whereas Esther's prayer had been granted immediately, Edith Stein, like Christ himself, was called to suffer a violent death. We know from different eyewitness accounts that, despite her fear, she approached the moment with serenity and calm. Bishop Pachowiak of Hildesheim has summarized the recollections of her final days:

> Surrounded by so much suffering, Edith Stein responded with boundless forbearance and overflowing love. In union with Christ, and as a share in the work of reparation, she willingly submitted to the brutal cruelty of her tormentors. She was absolutely convinced that atoning love alone is powerful enough to overcome the world's hatred. Others despaired and gave in to bitterness and hatred; she offered consolation and quiet encouragement and performed the humblest services for children, the sick, and the dying.[2]

Waltraud Herbstrith
Edith Stein Carmel
Tübingen
August 9, 1980
The thirty-eighth anniversary of Edith Stein's death

---

[2] Waltraud Herbstrith, *Bilder des Lebens-Edith Stein,* 2d ed. (Munich: Kaffke, 1982), p. 82.

Chapter 1

Childhood and Loss of Faith

Edith Stein was born in Breslau, Germany, on October 12, 1891, the youngest of eleven children of a devout Jewish family. Her ancestors from Posen and Upper Silesia, were hardworking, ambitious merchants, with large families nurtured on the spirit of the Psalms. They worshipped the God of Israel in synagogue and in private prayer at home. New Year's, the Day of Atonement, and Passover were the high points of the year. Supporting this Jewish tradition was a strong sense of communal awareness, fostered above all by the mother of the family. Father and children alike revered her authority. Edith Stein's great-grandfather on her mother's side had been cantor and leader of prayer in his congregation; his wife, a *mulier fortis*,[1] had lit the candles at the beginning of every Sabbath, using the words handed down from generation to generation: "Lord, do not burden us overmuch, but give us the burdens we are able to bear." The Steins accepted the problems and difficulties of the busy work week with patience and confidence in God's help. Parents taught their children to love the poor, to carry on the ancient tradition of dedicating the first fruits, and to respect the beliefs of others. One particularly impressive person was Edith Stein's grandmother, whose intelligent, sensitive face held a special attraction for the little girl. Her advice was frequently sought after; even among the nobility, it was considered an honor to count her as a friend.

---

[1] *Mulier fortis* is a woman of inner strength and authority. —TRANS.

Against this background the powerful figure of Edith Stein's mother stands out forcefully. Frau Auguste Stein was a woman accustomed to hard work from her childhood. Intelligent and energetic herself, she passed on these essential character traits to her youngest daughter. She was the formative influence in Edith Stein's development, the primary source of strength and affection for the growing child. No matter what difficulties she had to encounter, Frau Stein bore everything in union with God. She had lost four children in the first years of her marriage and experienced the problems of an expanding lumber business in Lublinitz. Financial difficulties following the firm's initial success had compelled the family to move to Breslau. This had demanded the sacrifice not only of home but, more importantly, of close ties with relatives. They had barely settled into Breslau when tragedy struck again. Herr Stein, aged forty-eight, died without warning on a business errand, leaving Frau Stein entirely responsible for the care of seven children and the management of a debt-ridden business. Edith Stein was not even two years old at the time.

It was Frau Stein's unshakable determination that carried the family through this period of trial. Disregarding her relatives' well-intentioned suggestions that she give up the lumber firm, she put her trust in God and continued to work to support the children. Edith, from that point on, always stood for her as her husband's last testament. Frau Stein never forgot the way the child had called her father back for a final goodbye as he set off for the work site in the woods, the scene of his fatal stroke. Furthermore, Edith Stein had been born on the Day of Atonement. She explains the significance of this fact in her autobiography:

> My mother laid great emphasis on the occurrence, and I think, more than anything else, it made her youngest child especially dear to her. . . . The Day of Atonement is the most solemn of all Jewish holidays, the day when the high priest entered the Holy of Holies, taking along the sacrifices to be offered in atonement for himself and all the people, after the scapegoat,

burdened with the sins of the nation, had been driven into the wilderness.[2]

Mother and daughter both regarded this coincidence as a mark of election. Neither one realized the cost of the atoning sacrifice that then lay far in the future.

One of the effects of Frau Stein's absorption in the lumber business and the cares of a large family was that Erna and Edith, the two youngest, grew up inseparable. Else, the oldest daughter, assisted Frau Stein with their upbringing—not a simple task at times. Edith in particular, despite her affectionate nature, was not easy to control. This is documented in the humorous account of her early years that she later composed. When things did not go her way, she confessed there, her normal vivacity would express itself by means of temper tantrums. Even locking her in her room did no good at such moments: she simply continued annoying the rest of the family by banging her fists against the door.

As a little girl, Edith Stein remembered, she always had to "put in her two cents" in the grown-ups' conversation and impress them with her clever remarks. A childhood friend recalled: "There was nothing extraordinary about her being precocious, considering she was the youngest of so many brothers and sisters. She read a lot and the others kept encouraging her, which was fine. But she also developed an uncontrollable vanity, and when she didn't reach her goal—to prove she was the best and the smartest—she vented her frustration in tears of rage. That wasn't so attractive."[3]

Edith Stein was clearly a high-strung, independent young child. She possessed a precocious mind and an unusual memory for poems and stories that made her seem something of a

---

[2] Edith Stein, *Aus dem Leben einer jüdischen Familie. Kindheit und Jugend,* Edith Steins Werke, Bd. VII (Louvain: Nauwelaerts/Freiburg: Herder, 1965), p. 41.

[3] Teresia Renata Posselt, *Edith Stein. Eine Grosse Frau unseres Jahrhunderts,* 9th ed. (Freiburg-Basel-Vienna: Herder, 1963), p. 10.

child prodigy. "But within me," she wrote, "another hidden world was emerging, where I would assimilate on my own the things that I saw and heard during the day."[4] At age seven, for no apparent reason, a change began to occur in the little girl. The temperamental young child turned into a quiet introvert. All her reliance on her sister Else and her closeness to her mother, who came first thing each night after work to kiss the child good-night, could not alleviate the isolation her awakening intellect experienced. She found herself living in a separate world inside herself, one that attracted her so powerfully that external impressions only provided the raw material for building it in private. As a result of the move inward, she suffered severely from loneliness right in the middle of a happy family life. "In spite of the great closeness between us," she wrote, "I couldn't confide in my mother more than in anyone else. From early childhood I led a strange double life that produced alternations of behavior which must have seemed incomprehensible and erratic to any outside observer."[5]

This double life had various consequences. Self-assertive temper tantrums were replaced by psychic fears and hypersensitivity. Inner defenses against impressions coming from the outside world were weakened to such an extent that seeing a drunken man on the street or hearing an unkind word casually spoken caused her intense suffering. Her constantly overstimulated imagination could no longer integrate the things she saw and heard. Often her body reacted with high fevers. But, "I never said a word about my secret sufferings to anyone. It just never occurred to me that you could talk about these things."[6]

She was particularly affected by an incident from this period involving dancing, which in addition to confirming her precocity revealed an unusual gift for empathy. It happened at a

---

[4] Stein, *Jüdische Familie*, p. 43.

[5] Ibid., p. 42.

[6] Ibid., p. 43.

large family gathering where she and Erna were dancing partners. Since the children had had little formal training, the dancing mistress placed them off to the side. She was all the more surprised, therefore, when she noticed Edith elegantly mimicking all her movements. Edith was soon the star of the evening, loaded down with praise and compliments. The dancing mistress went so far as to recommend that she study ballet, a suggestion Edith herself did not think worthy of "a serious answer". Back at home, however, the little ballerina had to face her brothers' and sisters' criticism for her flirtatious manner while dancing.

> Right from early childhood, my relatives used two qualities to describe me. They scolded me—correctly—for being vain, and they called me "Edith, the smart one" with an emphasis on "smart". Both of these hurt me very much. The second, because I thought they were saying that I tended to exaggerate my own intelligence. Also, even as a little girl, I knew it was much more important to be good than to be smart.[7]

Throughout her preadolescent years, Edith Stein was basically unaffected by either her mother's piety or her family's religious practices: any experience of God she had came in the form of her mother's love. When the shadows of her private world began to dissipate soon after, it was not in response to some personal awareness of God. The actual motives at work in making Edith Stein curb her high-strung nature and become calmer and more docile are characteristic and worth considering. There was, of course, the natural sensitivity the Stein children felt for their mother's abhorrence of anything sinful; never would they purposely do something to merit her disapproval. But in Edith Stein's case, what led her to discipline herself was the fear of forfeiting "her spiritual freedom and personal dignity" by "letting herself go". The young child recognized the degradation in compulsive passions that are

[7] Ibid., p. 86.

allowed to operate unchecked. In accord with the value she placed on freedom of spirit, she developed an amazing firmness of character. "Very early on I acquired so much self-control that I could remain constantly even-tempered without any great struggle."[8] This firmness of will and fidelity to the truth the moment she recognized it proved to be the decisive elements in molding her personality. No wonder the elder brothers and sisters came to very different conclusions about the two youngest siblings. Whereas Erna seemed as "transparent as water" to them, they considered Edith "a book with seven seals".

With growth in self-awareness, the precocious child's anxieties more and more transformed themselves into dreams of a brilliant future. Edith Stein believed that she was called to greatness. Her awakening mind desired to break the hold of her extravagant imagination and attain to freedom and recognition. She found it humiliating to be a child surrounded by unsympathetic adults and yearned for an environment where she could learn and be able to express herself. Obviously, it was school that she wanted. As she later wrote, "In school people took me seriously."[9] School in fact turned out to be the place where she received the freedom she craved.

Several years earlier, at the age of six, she had insisted with almost unbelievable obstinacy on being admitted to the Victoria School in Breslau prior to the regular entrance date. Kindergarten she had categorically refused to consider, as something beneath her dignity. She had even agreed to do without presents on her sixth birthday on condition that she be allowed to attend school. Else Stein, then a teacher at the school, managed to have Edith admitted in mid-year. It took Edith only a few months to catch up with the rest of the pupils; from then on, she steadily maintained her position at the head of the class. How much her active mind needed the influence

[8] Ibid., p. 44.
[9] Ibid., p. 47.

of a formal education can be judged from her own words: "School played a major role in our childhood. I could almost say I felt more at home there than in my own house."[10] It is a surprisingly emphatic statement, considering her strong sense of family.

The school in the Ritterplatz, once the Schaffgottsche Palace, rapidly became a second home. She was already largely familiar with everything from the stories her brothers and sisters had told, so she found no problem adjusting to the new routine. It was a case of a life she had previously experienced in her imagination, "in her own depths", taking on a solid form of its own.

At school, the young pupil came to appreciate the opportunity for expressing her inner world in essays and compositions without needing to fear the condescending smiles of grown-ups. She "swallowed" her textbooks like someone starved, in German and history above all. Even when her hair was being combed at home, she kept on reading, showing somewhat less enthusiasm in carrying out her ordinary household tasks. Though later Edith Stein was to regret this one-sided development, for the most part it was neither vanity nor competitiveness that drove her on, but the need to supply her mind with sufficient nourishment. "Little by little, things started getting brighter and clearer in my inner world."[11] As a result of her exposure to education, she succeeded in orienting her intellectual faculties to the outside world, while her imagination discovered new outlets in experience and reading. Erna Stein summarized those elementary school years in these words: "Since it was not customary at the time to begin the school year in autumn, she had only half a year in the beginners' class. By Christmas, however, she was already one of the best pupils. She was just as gifted as she was hard-working, with a will of iron. Yet she was never competitive in the bad

---

[10] Ibid., p. 35.
[11] Ibid., p. 44.

sense of the word. She was a good classmate, always ready to help out."[12]

This made it all the more surprising when at thirteen the strong-willed, gifted young girl announced that she wanted to leave school. Perhaps her frail constitution and a resulting psychological and mental exhaustion contributed to the unexpected decision. The collapse of her childhood faith may also have been a factor. Edith Stein acknowledged years later that from thirteen to twenty-one she could not believe in the existence of a personal God.

Erna Stein described the effect of Edith's decision on her family: "Since Edith had done so brilliantly all the way through school, we all took it for granted that when she finished, she would take the new college-preparatory course with me at the Victoria School and from there go on to the university. But she shocked us instead with her decision to leave school. My mother went along with it, due to the fact that Edith had always been small and delicate."[13]

Edith was sent to recuperate at the home of her sister Else in Hamburg. Else, now married to a doctor and the mother of three children, greatly appreciated the help. "She stayed on for eight months, conscientiously and tirelessly doing everything that was asked of her, even though housework had no great attraction for her."[14]

In these few words, all of Edith Stein's essential traits can be perceived: a ready intelligence, an iron will, a strong sense of duty, and a natural desire to be of help. Though in her own opinion she may still have been quiet and reserved, absorbed in her own private world, in Hamburg she proved herself to be quite capable of efficiently handling practical responsibilities. When Frau Stein came to take her home, she found Edith thriving and blossoming into womanhood.

---

[12] Posselt, *Edith Stein,* p. 14.
[13] Ibid.
[14] Ibid.

Evidently, the few months of practical work had helped resolve the crisis. Yet a certain degree of inner uncertainty persisted back in Breslau; despite Edith's growth in self-confidence, she seemed unable to decide on a new direction for her life. It was her mother who came to the rescue with the suggestion that she return to school. To this Edith had no objection. She felt her earlier interest in intellectual pursuits restored, thanks to her new-found vitality. With enthusiasm she plunged into the study of Latin and mathematics. From now on, she told herself, teaching would be her goal.

> I still remember that half year of continual work as the first completely happy period in my life. For the first time, my intellectual powers were functioning at full capacity, at a task which was truly worthy of them. As soon as I sat down at my desk, in a room reserved for my use, the rest of the world ceased to exist. Every time I finished a math problem, I would whistle a few notes, like a song of triumph. But I never even thought of going on in mathematics: that wasn't what I had been born for. With Latin, it was a different story. I had never enjoyed learning any modern language nearly as much. Latin grammar fascinated me with its strict rules. It was like learning my native tongue. Back then I had no idea that it was the language of the Church and that someday I would be praying in it. [15]

After this brief but intense period of private preparation, Edith Stein passed the admission exam for the eleventh grade. She was back in her native element, having visibly benefitted from the time away. The childhood exuberance and know-it-all attitude had moderated to a quiet yet cheerful reserve, destined to serve as the foundation for her powers of inner endurance. A schoolmate observed: "She worked very hard without being pushy or competitive; even then, there was a real quality of reserve about her. I always thought that she was

[15] Stein, *Jüdische Familie,* p. 97.

older than us and not just smarter, probably because she seemed more serious and mature than the rest of us. I remember her as a quiet, thoughtful, and truly likable person."[16]

For Edith Stein, returning to school meant returning to a world without God. Now that her depression was overcome, she was eager to continue the search for the ultimate grounds of being, the quest for truth taking the place of childhood faith. With this in mind, she adapted her mother's religious example—the long prayers in synagogue, the selfless love of her children, the twenty-four-hour fast on the Day of Atonement—as a basis for her own ethical behavior. As a result, the young student discovered that, much as she liked receiving the prizes bestowed at the annual awards assembly, she equally disliked attracting attention to herself or having to discuss her personal accomplishments. Furthermore, she found herself committed to transforming those "brilliant hopes for the future" into objective achievements, capable of standing on their own merit. On one occasion she startled a classmate with the statement, "A translator must be like a windowpane, which lets through all the light but itself remains unseen."[17] All this indicates how much the fifteen-year-old Edith had matured. Edith Stein also learned how to be a good friend, developing an attractive social side to balance out her scholarly interests. People liked her for her even temper, her trustworthiness, and her good judgment. As Erna Stein recalled: "She took an active part in all social activities, along with the schoolwork. She was never a killjoy of any sort. You could tell her all your worries and problems, and she would always be ready to offer advice and assistance. Then somehow everything would usually turn out for the best."[18]

Edith Stein's talent for abstract thinking did not prevent her from taking an active interest in the world of living things.

---

[16] Posselt, *Edith Stein*, p. 15.
[17] Ibid.
[18] Ibid.

The future phenomenologist had a passionate love for nature in all its manifestations. As a city girl, she took special pleasure in spending vacations in the country, from which she would return filled with enthusiastic reports of hikes through fields and meadows where, as she claimed, her spirit could breathe more freely. All she had to do was to pass by a running stream on a country walk with Erna and she would run to scoop up the fish in her hands.

Holiday trips to relatives in Lublinitz gave the same joy to the teenagers. In this prosperous little city, Edith's gift for observation found a fertile field. Her quick, good-natured intelligence took in everything: the mysterious treasures at her uncle's business, her aunt's affectionate and well-intentioned scoldings, the evening discussions, the games she joined in with her cousins. A friend of hers, Rose Bluhm, described her at that time:

> I got to know Edith during our last years together at the Victoria. Both of us were taking private lessons in German literature from a wonderful blind woman, so I came to know her pretty well. I vividly remember what a delightful girl Edith was, so warm-hearted and vivacious and with a marvelous sense of humor. When she laughed, her beautiful gray eyes would shine. She also had a dimple on her chin which we all found charming.[19]

Unfortunately, despite the sense of closeness between Frau Stein and her family in Lublinitz (which she always thought of as home), contact with relatives grew considerably less frequent due to a fundamental difference in outlook. Frau Stein was repelled by the increasingly pervasive moral liberalism around her, while most of the relatives regarded her strictness with her daughters as backward and overly idealistic. Consequently, Frau Stein felt most comfortable within her own home.

[19] Edith-Stein-Archiv, Karmel Köln.

As graduation approached, it was clear that on account of the family's straitened circumstances, Erna and Edith would have to work toward a profession. Luckily, with the older children already employed, there was still the possibility of university studies. Though such studies continued to be a rarity for women in that era, a privilege that only the most talented could aspire to, Edith Stein was determined to go on to teaching. Her initial desire to imitate her sister Else had taken on the character of an inner necessity. At seventeen, she had begun to tutor a number of her classmates for the sheer joy of teaching and had demonstrated all the requisites of a good educator: tact, authority, patience, love of the material, and the gift for getting along with other people, particularly young ones. But there was a test of another kind which Edith Stein would have to pass before she could begin her studies at the university. Her uncle David, a well-to-do apothecary in Chemnitz, had worked out plans of his own for his talented nieces. He wanted to establish a sanatorium where Edith and Erna would function as the doctors on his staff. To sweeten his offer, the druggist frequently invited "the doctors" on boating parties and car trips, while his wife worked alongside him to turn the pretty young girls into socially acceptable young ladies. No doubt the two students enjoyed the time spent with the childless couple; nevertheless, as far as Edith was concerned, Uncle David's plans could not unsettle her. With the same quiet imperturbability that years before had driven a cousin to scream, "Why can't *I* be right for once?"[20] she stood her ground with her uncle. All attempts to change her mind were in vain. Uncle David had underestimated his gentle, lovable niece. "I could not proceed with anything except on the basis of some inner drive. My decisions emerged from a level of depth which I myself was unable to grasp clearly. But once something had emerged into consciousness and taken on a definite shape in my mind, then nothing could hold me back.

[20] Stein, *Jüdische Familie,* pp. 36–37.

Then it became almost a game to accomplish the apparently impossible."[21]

Realizing that Erna was less opposed to the notion of medical school, Edith Stein advised her to follow her own conscience. As she explained to her uncle, each person has a responsibility for selecting the career that most truly corresponds to his inclinations and abilities. In her own case, teaching was the only choice. While the apothecary was not convinced by such modern ideas, he respected his niece's independent thinking all the same. He had more luck with Erna, who set aside her strong interest in languages to take him up on his suggestion. Though no joint sanatorium ever was established, Erna Stein eventually became a highly qualified doctor.

At twenty, with the *Abitur*[22] just completed, Edith Stein was a young woman of determination and a clear sense of direction. This is apparent from the reflection she made on her choice of career, once the pressure of the *Abitur* was behind her:

> After the exams, instead of the great sense of happiness that I had expected, there was only a great inward emptiness. I saw a pleasant and familiar way of life disappearing forever. And what now? I thought about my uncle's unspoken objections to my choice of career and wondered if I had really made the right decision. I knew we were in the world to serve mankind. But wouldn't I do that best if I worked at something I had the appropriate talents for? The way I saw it, there was nothing to be said against my decision.[23]

Over the last few years, Edith Stein had been eagerly watching the intellectual revolution going on in industrialized society, so critically important for the transformation and

[21] Ibid., p. 94.

[22] The *Abitur* are the comprehensive exams taken at the end of one's secondary education. —TRANS.

[23] Ibid., p. 114.

determination of the future role of women. She had recognized the problems it was generating and had committed herself to an active part in their solution. In choosing teaching as her career, far from acting from financial motives or the desire for a respected place in society, she was corresponding with an inner law that she believed was imposed on every individual.

Chapter 2

From Psychology to Philosophy

From the external point of view, Edith Stein's life remained unchanged when she entered the University of Breslau in March 1911. Relations with her immediate family, relatives, and friends continued as before. She was still set on teaching as her intended career and registered for the required courses in German and history. Soon, however, another subject began to divert much of the young atheist's attention away from her professional courses. She started to attend lectures in psychology, hoping to discover through this discipline the underlying coherence of human existence. Since it was the soul as center of the human person that appeared to her as the fundamental problem, she decided that the study of experimental psychology would best help her along the way to truth. She enrolled in the courses of psychologists such as Honigwald and Stern and prepared to write seminar papers for them from the viewpoint of cognitive psychology. But what she discovered disappointed her. She found herself confronted with a quantitative approach based on the methods of the natural sciences, determined to prove that the soul she was investigating did not exist at all. In this "psychology without a soul", "spirit, meaning, and life" had all been eliminated from the current of psychological existence; the decision whether or not a spiritual unity should be posited beneath man's sense impressions was left to the individual. The entire notion of the soul had been relegated to the realm of the irrational and mythological, henceforth to be regarded with a skeptical smile.

Edith Stein remained unconvinced. As she continued on with her research, she came upon the book destined to revolutionize her intellectual life: the *Logical Investigations* of the phenomenologist Edmund Husserl. What this epoch-making work offered her first and foremost was an answer to her search for clarifying first principles. Husserl was struggling toward a rediscovery of "Spirit", toward a purified knowledge, freed from conceptual apparatus, which could get at the being of things through an intuitive perception of their essence. This was inspiration for Edith Stein. Soon it was her professors, amazed by her grasp of phenomenology, who were asking her opinion in the seminar sessions.

From then on, Edith Stein wanted to leave Breslau to pursue her studies with Husserl in Göttingen. As she noted in her diary: "In my fourth semester, I came to feel that Breslau had nothing more to offer me and that my studies needed a greater stimulus. Something was pushing me to move on. . . . I didn't know anyone capable of advising me, so I blithely went about looking for my own way myself."[1]

Perhaps, then, it was an unconscious fear of the unknown that led Edith Stein to request a dissertation topic from Professor Stern prior to her departure from Breslau. However, no sooner had she received the theme—"Children's Thought Processes Examined through the Interview Method"—than she realized that she could never be content working with the meager research methods currently available to psychology. She put the case forcefully:

> The sole result of all my psychological study had been to convince me that the science was still in its infancy and that it possessed neither the required foundation of refined first principles nor the capacity to formulate them on its own. This is why everything I had learned so far about phenomenology delighted

[1] Edith Stein, *Aus dem Leben einer jüdischen Familie. Kindheit und Jugend,* Edith Steins Werke, Bd. VII (Louvain: Nauwelaerts/Freiburg: Herder, 1965), pp. 146 and 123.

me, because it consisted precisely in this task of clarification where, right from the start, you yourself forged the necessary intellectual equipment.[2]

The same Edith Stein who as a child had eagerly gone on walks to places "she had never been before" now was attracted by phenomenology's independent procedure and by the newness of the field.

Edith Stein's desire caught her family by surprise. Although both she and Erna had at one time considered the possibility of spending a semester in romantic Heidelberg, the sisters had dropped the idea on practical grounds. Erna had had to give first thought to the preparations for her comprehensives, and as for Edith, the family's tight financial situation had seemed to rule out the chances of a temporary transfer. All the more unexpected came the wholehearted backing of Frau Stein. If she had any objection at all, it was only to the few months' separation from her youngest child. "My mother said: If it's necessary for your studies, I don't want to stand in your way. You do what you think is right; you're the best judge of that. But she was sad—much sadder than a one-semester separation should have made her."[3]

Unable to see where her daughter's intellectual development would lead, the mother nonetheless sensed an impending ideological split. Frau Stein knew that Edith had turned away from the God of her fathers. Her piety had not succeeded in effectively resisting the inroads liberal thinking had made on the family's traditions and customs. It was true that all the children continued to revere their mother and that Edith in particular faithfully accompanied her to synagogue. But, "what actually edified her was her mother's complete absorption in God rather than any of the religious ceremonies".[4]

[2] Ibid., p. 150.

[3] Ibid., pp. 123 and 147.

[4] Teresia Renata Posselt, *Edith Stein. Eine Grosse Frau unseres Jahrhunderts,* 9th ed. (Freiburg-Basel-Vienna: Herder, 1963), p. 16.

Edith Stein herself, for all her excitement and anticipation, did not fail to see the significance of the approaching separation. "Secretly in my heart of hearts I knew that the separation would be a drastic one."[5] She realized that in leaving behind her native Breslau, she was leaving the world of Judaism and the Law as well. But her mind was made up. "Here, as later on, one slight movement was sufficient to sever the most apparently unbreakable ties—and then I was off, like a bird which has escaped from the fowler's net."[6]

Shortly before her departure for Göttingen, Edith Stein went to say good-bye to Hugo Hermsen, the organizer of a pedagogical study group whose meetings she attended. He said to her in farewell, "I hope in Göttingen you'll find people who measure up to your standards."[7] The words not only surprised her, they left her feeling somewhat stunned.

> I wasn't used to being corrected by anyone anymore. At home, nobody dared to say a word to me, and my friends kept me surrounded with love and admiration. I was living in the naive delusion common to so many people with no faith but with an exalted ethical idealism: that since I found goodness attractive, I personally must be good myself. I had always considered it my right to take exception to anything that struck me negatively, sometimes, even, in a mocking and ironic way. There were actually people who considered me "delightfully malicious". So, to hear such serious parting words from a man I respected and loved came to me as a painful shock. I didn't get angry with him over them or try to dismiss them as unjust criticism. Instead, they were like a trumpet call which forced me to start thinking.[8]

Once arrived in Göttingen, Edith Stein quickly settled into her new environment. It was an entirely new world for her,

[5] Stein, *Jüdische Familie*, p. 149.
[6] Ibid., p. 146.
[7] Ibid., p. 130.
[8] Ibid.

and she entered it filled with hope. "I was twenty-one and all excited over everything that was going to happen to me. Dear old Göttingen! I think only people who were there between 1905 and 1914, in the brief flowering of the Göttingen School of phenomenology, can appreciate what that name contains for us."[9]

In her diary entries of that initial period, some of the magic the old university town worked on her can still be recaptured. Here she is seen openly and spontaneously relating with her fellow students, enjoying the experiences the surrounding locale provided in such abundance. She loved jotting down humorous stories about the easy-going citizens and their well-tended, historic little city. Nothing escaped her observer's eye. It wasn't long before she had thoroughly mastered her new setting, proving herself a born phenomenologist by the interest she showed in everything around her. Her classmate Rose Bluhm-Guttmann later wrote of those days:

We spent a wonderful summer semester together in Göttingen. I studied mathematics and philosophy; so did Edith, along with history. Back at the university, a number of us had become inseparable. Lilli Berg-Platau, a very old and dear friend of mine, was studying medicine there and so had got to be friends with Erna Stein, while Edith and I were both enrolled together in the philosophical faculty.

Though all of us took our work seriously, we still managed to find time for the things young people enjoy. We went on wonderful trips in the mountains, we danced, and we put together lovely musical evenings and special skits. For the holidays, the four of us—Lilli, Edith, Erna, and I—would always get together. Erna and Lilli would rent one room and Edith and I would rent another. The two of us used to stay up late every night talking, after having spent most of the day reading—philosophy above all, which interested both of us very much. We often went on marvelous hiking trips in the Harz mountains

9 Ibid., p. 165.

and in Thuringia; many a weekend was spent walking with our knapsacks in the Weser mountains.

Not only did we take all the same seminars in philosophy and education, we also worked together for the Democratic Party (women at that time still didn't have the vote), and both followed with great interest anything that concerned the subject of women's careers.

We shared a lovely little apartment with a bedroom, study, and cooking privileges too, if I remember correctly. Dinner we ate out but made our own breakfast and supper. Edith could cook and clean as well as I. She was the most gifted woman I have ever met in my life—and I have known many extraordinary women.

At the university, we were among the first women they admitted, so I think we formed a fairly select group. Edith had a deep love for truth. She had a penetrating and creative mind that kept on working at a problem until the truth came to light. [10]

Such, according to the reminiscences of a friend, was the nature of Edith Stein's early student life, in both its serious and its lighter aspects.

Edith Stein had come to Göttingen in the hope of discovering a new spiritual orientation. She was destined to spend years here as a disciple of Edmund Husserl and have her thinking exposed to a number of critical new influences. The magnet that had first attracted her to the city was the figure of the "Master", the pioneer of a revolutionary method of phenomenological research. Husserl, she had recognized, was pointing in the very direction she had previously searched for in modern philosophy in vain: the shift to the truth of the entities. Utterly disillusioned with a psychology that seemed unable to provide itself with a solid intellectual grounding, Edith Stein had felt compelled to search for truth in a philosophical formulation. This is precisely what Husserl's shift to the "phenomena", the various manifestations of being, promised her.

[10] Edith-Stein-Archiv, Karmel Köln.

Husserl had made the old, despised term "ontology" respectable once more, just at the hour when the so-called " 'Christian philosophy' was awaking like Sleeping Beauty from its centuries-old sleep."[11] Through postulating an a priori knowledge of essences, he had at one and the same time taken up arms against empiricism, skepticism, and relativism. Enthusiastic young realists had flocked to him, thus creating the "Göttingen School".

By the time Edith Stein arrived in 1913, the golden age of the Göttingen School had already passed. Its most notable representatives—Adolf Reinach, Hedwig Conrad-Martius, Alexander Koyré, Dietrich von Hildebrand, and Johannes Hering—had moved on and become either university professors or independent philosophers. Nonetheless, the spirit of Husserl continued to permeate the atmosphere: even the man on the street spontaneously spoke in terms of "phenomena". Edith Stein felt a little awed at the prospect of meeting such a personage. She knew that his students referred to him as "the Master" (although he himself rejected the title). But the ice was broken at their first introduction, when she told him that she had read the entire second volume of the *Logical Investigations*. With a smile Husserl responded, "The entire second volume? Now, *that* I call heroic!"[12] From then on, she had a place in the circle of Husserl's students.

Edith Stein plunged with zeal into the new studies. Energetic as ever, she immediately volunteered to keep the complex minutes of the seminar sessions, surprising her fellow students with her readiness and skill in argumentation. Because of the empathetic manner with which she approached Husserl's thought, she quickly became the student most sensitive to his intention. Edith Stein had come to Husserl searching for truth, and now in his seminars she learned that,

[11] Edith Stein, *Endliches und Ewiges Sein. Versuch eines Aufstiegs zum Sinn des Seins*, Edith Steins Werke, Bd. II (Louvain: Nauwelaerts/Freiburg: Herder, 1962), p. 6.

[12] Stein, *Jüdische Familie*, p. 174.

"knowledge, as the name implies, depends on knowing. . . . It is in knowing that we possess the truth."[13] By "truth", Husserl meant the "luminous certainty" that something is or is not so, sharply distinct from both ordinary opinion and blind conviction. Husserl wanted to overcome skepticism through the construction of a pure substantive meaning. His belief was that philosophy practiced as a rigorous science would lead to the discovery of truth. He appreciated the passive function of the intellect, its capacity for receiving truth from objects; and this insight, with its clear affinity to scholasticism, aroused widespread interest in his phenomenological method. As a teacher, Husserl trained his students to look at everything with strict impartiality and do away with their rationalist blinders. His open and dynamic method of procedure engendered an atmosphere in which intellectual friendships easily flourished. In fact, without being aware of it, Husserl was founding an intellectual movement that eventually would result in the conversion of many of his students to Christianity.

Hedwig Conrad-Martius, who became a close friend of Edith Stein's during this period, testified to the far-reaching effects that Husserl's outlook had on his students:

> Our commonly held approach to thinking and investigating created a bond among Husserl's students that can only be described as the natural outgrowth of a common spirit. I don't mean that we all had any private terminology or held to one individual system—not at all. It was, rather, our newly won insight into the intellectual attainability of Being in all its possible configurations that united us . . . , the ethos of objective purity and cleanliness . . . which rubbed off on our attitude, character and behavior. . . . This is what made it natural for all of us to become friends, without anyone giving a thought to somebody's social class, race or religion. Edith Stein was a born phenomenologist. Her calm, clear, and impartial thinking, her

[13] Edmund Husserl, *Logische Untersuchungen,* Bd. I (Halle: Verlag Niemeyer, 1913), p. 12.

undistorted vision, and her absolute objectivity all predestined her for it.[14]

Edith Stein continued studying history along with her work in philosophy. History helped broaden her horizons; it provided her with an arena for exercising her phenomenological talents as well as for developing her moral conscience.

My love for history was not a romantic escape into the past. It was closely bound up with a passionate involvement in present-day politics—in history in the making. Both of these interests stemmed from an unusually strong sense of social responsibility on my part—a feeling for the solidarity of mankind and also of its smaller communities. Repellent as Darwinian nationalism was to me, I had always been convinced of the significance and inborn historical necessity of having individual states with peoples and nations of distinct character. This was the reason socialist ideologies and international movements had never been able to gain any hold on me. As time went on, I found myself gradually moving away from the liberal notions I had grown up with and moving toward a more positive concept of the state, one which resembled conservatism but without a specific commitment to its Prussian form.

Besides these purely theoretical considerations, I felt personally grateful to the state which had given me free access to the sciences of culture by guaranteeing my right to an education. . . . Most of my fellow students displayed an indifference toward public affairs that shocked me. Some of them during the first few semesters went to the lectures only when they felt like it; others never worried about anything except obtaining the necessary information for exams and getting a good job later on. My own strong sense of social responsibility led me to an active participation in the struggle for women's suffrage. This was an issue that the bourgeois woman's movement still had not committed itself to. The Prussian Association for Women's Suffrage, which my friends and I had joined because it did insist on full political equality for women,

[14] Hedwig Conrad-Martius in *Edith Stein, Briefe an Hedwig Conrad-Martius* (Munich: Kösel-Verlag, 1960), pp. 62–65.

was mostly composed of socialists. All my friends were also
members of the League for School Reform. We went to all the
meetings together.[15]

Edith Stein listened enthusiastically to the lectures given by
Ranke's disciple Max Lehmann, whose "European way of
thinking" delighted her. It made her proud to think that
through Lehmann she was entering into the line of the great
historian. Yet justice remained her first concern, and when Lehmann occasionally took gratuitous swipes at Prussia (he himself preferred English imperialism to its German form), it only
confirmed her in her devotion to the Prussian system. Her goal
in these historical studies was to reach an understanding of the
unity of the human person. The importance she placed on intellectual history in this regard can be gathered from the following statement:

> Only the individual who experiences himself as a person, as an
> integrated whole, is capable of understanding other persons.
> Yet, at the same time, we fully appreciate Ranke's desire to
> "extinguish" himself in order to see things as they really were.
> . . . The self is the individual's way of structuring experience.
> The great master of understanding recognized it as the primary
> source of delusion and a potentially dangerous threat. By
> adopting it as a standard of measurement, we can lock our-
> selves up in our own individuality. Then other people become
> riddles for us, or worse yet, we can mold them into our own
> image and thus distort the historical truth.[16]

Edith Stein longed to achieve such a "mastery of understanding", to transcend the selfish constraints the ego imposes
and arrive through a process of empathy at an objective set of
values. She decided to approach Husserl with a theme for a
doctoral dissertation, intending to investigate the nature of

[15] Stein, *Jüdische Familie*, pp. 125, 126, 127.
[16] Edith Stein, *Zum Problem der Einfühlung*, doctoral dissertation (Halle,
1917; reprinted Munich: Kaffke, 1980), p. 129.

empathy in depth. Comprehensives, she felt, could wait until a later time. What was certain was that she could not leave Göttingen. Too many internal changes had taken place since her arrival "for one semester". "The closer it came to the end of the semester, the less I could accept the idea of leaving for good. The last few months hadn't been a little interlude. They had marked the beginning of a new phase in my life."[17] For all her determination, she wondered how she could explain the situation to her family. Hadn't it been enough of a sacrifice for her mother to send her to Göttingen for one semester? Unexpectedly, Professor Lehmann came to the rescue. He was so impressed with the paper she had written for his history seminar that he recommended she expand it into the written portion of her comprehensives. The offer was too good to be refused. Although it would necessitate a further revision of plans, now it would be easy to persuade her family in Breslau that she ought to stay on in Göttingen.

When Edith Stein spoke to Husserl about a dissertation topic, he was astounded. "Are you really that far along already?" he asked. Husserl was accustomed to having doctoral students spend years preparing their theses, and he categorically insisted that they pass the comprehensives before he would allow them to begin. To his mind, a thorough acquaintance with the methods of other disciplines was indispensable for the study of philosophy. This came as a disappointment to Edith Stein, who had intended to tackle the dissertation right away. Nonetheless, she agreed to all his conditions, grateful that she would be able to remain in Göttingen. She began to formulate her immediate plans:

> If I had to do the comprehensives before the doctorate [she wrote in her diary], I wanted to get it out of the way as soon as possible. Five semesters of university study were already behind me, but I couldn't register for the exams yet since the prescribed minimum was six. This was a requirement that dated

[17] Stein, *Jüdische Familie,* p. 190.

from the old days when there had been less material to cover. Nowadays, most people were taking six to eight semesters. Personally, I felt that was out of the question. I had made up my mind—that winter I would have to finish the draft for my study on empathy and make enough headway preparing for the orals that I could register for the exam at the end of the semester.[18]

[18] Ibid., p. 191.

Chapter 3

What Is Truth?

In 1913, Husserl published *Ideas: Toward a Pure Phenomenology and Phenomenological Method.* Reflecting on its consequences, Edith Stein later wrote:

> The main reason the *Logical Investigations* had made such an impact was that they seemed to mark a radical break with critical idealism, both of the Kantian and neo-Kantian types. The book had been considered as representing a "new form of scholasticism", because it transferred the attention away from the subject and back onto the object. Once again perception was treated as something receptive, governed by its objects, rather than constitutive and regulative of the objects as in critical philosophy. All the young phenomenologists were committed realists.
>
> In *Ideas,* however, a number of expressions cropped up which seemed to indicate a reversion to idealism on the part of the author. Nothing he said to us by way of explanation was able to allay our suspicions. It was the beginning of an evolution in Husserl's thought that would lead him increasingly to identify "transcendental idealism" as the real core of his philosophy and to expend all his energy in laying its theoretical foundations. His old Göttingen students could not support him in this move, to his regret and theirs.[1]

---

[1] Edith Stein, *Aus dem Leben einer jüdischen Familie. Kindheit und Jugend,* Edith Steins Werke, Bd. VII (Louvain: Nauwelaerts/Freiburg: Herder, 1965), p. 174.

Edith Stein wondered if she herself could continue in this philosophical direction any longer. She felt her idealistic faith in philosophy being shaken, much as her attraction to experimental psychology had been a number of years before. One thing she had to admit: "philosophy as a rigorous science" did not seem to be living up to its own strict standards: "In its present state [it was] still a fragment and, as such, subject to all the errors, false starts, and distortions that hinder the human mind in its endeavors."[2] Two philosophers whom Edith Stein came to know during these years proved to be of decisive significance in gradually leading her to this realization.

In Göttingen, she was introduced to the phenomenologist Max Scheler. His "prophetic philosophy" made an indelible impression on her. Scheler was a Jewish convert from Munich and, at the time Edith Stein attended his lectures, filled with admiration for the spiritual beauty of Catholicism. His *Formalism in Ethics and a Material Ethic of Values* was exerting a stronger influence in philosophical circles than Husserl's *Ideas*. Young phenomenologists rallied around him. In contrast to the matter-of-factness of Husserl, Scheler had something infatuating about him: "Never again [wrote Edith Stein] would I experience in such pure form the 'phenomenon of creative genius'. The brightness of a higher realm shone from his large blue eyes. He had a beautiful face with finely chiselled features, marked by the ravages life had inflicted."[3]

Scheler's impassioned intuition and his "feeling for values" (*Wertfühlen*),[4] which breaks through all systems, concepts, and a priori notions to reveal the fullness of being to "the seeing eye and the empathetic heart", introduced Edith Stein to a hitherto unknown world. His recent discovery of Christianity

[2] Edith Stein, *Endliches und Ewiges Sein. Versuch eines Aufstiegs zum Sinn des Seins,* Edith Steins Werke, Bd. II (Louvain: Nauwelaerts/Freiburg: Herder, 1962), pp. 16, 17.

[3] Stein, *Jüdische Familie,* p. 182.

[4] Erich Przywara, S.J., "Edith Stein", *In und Gegen* (Nuremberg: Verlag Glock und Lutz, 1955), p. 49.

in particular exposed her to fresh data which, as a phenomenologist, she was bound to consider. In the words of a friend:

> At that time, the Munich phenomenologist was holding a se-
> ries of evening lectures in Göttingen on religious questions—
> for instance, "The Nature of the Holy". This counted as quite
> an event in the little university town and may well have been
> the stimulus behind the movement toward the Catholic
> Church undeniably taking place among Husserl's and Rein-
> ach's students. Both of us were affected by the excitement as
> well. We still were "children of this world" back then. Neither
> one of us ever mentioned the possibility of changing religion.
> But for me, and I think for her too, it provided the first push
> along the road to conversion.[5]

Scheler demonstrated with irresistible brilliance that religion alone makes the human being human. He placed humility
at the foundation of all moral endeavor and argued that the sole
purpose of this endeavor was to lead the individual to the loss
of self in God—and on to new resurrection. Edith Stein had
never heard anyone speak like that before. Yet rather than succumbing to the power of his oratory, she found herself deeply
affected by the truth of his statements. "It was my first contact
with a world that until then had been completely unfamiliar.
I can't say that it led me directly to faith. But it did open up a
whole new realm of 'phenomena' that I wouldn't be able to
pass by blindly anymore."[6] She came away from the confrontation with Christianity forced to acknowledge her own spiritual poverty and wondering if there might be an "External"
which manifests itself in the world of objects.

One of Edith Stein's friends in Göttingen was Eduard Metis, an Orthodox Jew. They had taken a course in German literature together, in which they had read Ulfilas' medieval
German version of the Gospels. She recalled that, "a little

[5] Teresia Renata Posselt, *Edith Stein. Eine Grosse Frau unseres Jahrhunderts,*
9th ed. (Freiburg-Basel-Vienna: Herder, 1963), p. 47.
[6] Stein, *Jüdische Familie,* p. 183.

while later in Göttingen when I began to interest myself in religious questions, I wrote to Metis asking him for his idea of
God and whether he himself believed in a personal God. The
answer was brief: God is Spirit—there is nothing more to be
said. To me it was as if I had been given a stone instead of
bread."[7]

"Whenever we come into contact with realms of value that
we cannot enter, we become aware of our own deficient value
and unworthiness."[8] In these words taken from the doctoral
dissertation she was then researching, Edith Stein showed that
she had begun to identify with the Schelerian human being
who prays and searches for God. Scheler had taken the blind-
fold from her eyes and she would not flee from the reality she
saw revealed.

> All that constant drilling about looking at everything without
> prejudice and throwing away our blinders hadn't been in vain.
> The bars of the rationalist prejudices I had unconsciously
> grown up with collapsed, and there, standing in front of me,
> was the world of faith. I could see that among the inhabitants
> were people whom I admired, people whom I worked with on
> a day-to-day basis. That made it worth some serious reflection
> at the very least.[9]

One of the people whom Edith Stein admired was the lecturer Adolf Reinach. He was Husserl's most valued colleague,
as well as the link between the Master and his students, due to
an ability to relate with people that Husserl lacked. Studying
with him, "we were not passive learners listening to someone
teach. We were involved in a common search with an expert
guide to direct us."[10]

[7] Ibid., p. 142.

[8] Edith Stein, *Zum Problem der Einfühlung*, doctoral dissertation (Halle,
1917; reprinted Munich: Kaffke, 1980), p. 130.

[9] Stein, *Jüdische Familie*, p. 183.

[10] Ibid., p. 195.

All the young phenomenologists were deeply affected by their contact with the scholar. Hedwig Conrad-Martius called him "our dearly loved younger teacher, one of the founding phenomenologists". Edith Stein was also profoundly influenced by her friendship with Reinach and his wife. In him she discovered someone who practiced what Scheler preached. As she wrote of their initial interview: "Our first conversation . . . left me very happy and filled with a deep sense of gratitude. Never before could I remember meeting anybody so absolutely good-hearted. Naturally, I expected that love would be shown me by my relatives and close friends. But here was something entirely different. It was my first glimpse into a totally new world."[11]

In the winter following the idyllic experience of her first semester in Göttingen, Edith Stein entered a period of intense loneliness and hard work. Her friends had gone home from Göttingen; her philosophical questions weighed on her like a nightmare. Moods of despair tormented her, which she described years later in these words:

> I was having my first experience of what I was destined to come up against in all future attempts at writing: until I had come to some clarity in my own mind regarding the issue at hand, books were completely useless to me. This struggle for clarity went on amid great internal suffering which never gave me a moment's peace day or night. I even forgot what it meant to get a good night's sleep; it was years before I was able to sleep soundly again.
>
> Bit by bit, I worked myself into a real state of despair. It was the first time in my life that I had ever confronted anything that I couldn't master by sheer force of will. Unconsciously my mother's sayings—"Where there's a will, there's a way" and "God helps those who help themselves"—had taken deep root in me. Before this, I had always prided myself on having a head that was tougher than the thickest wall. But I had made my

[11] Ibid., p. 173.

head sore from running into this one, and the stubborn wall still wouldn't give.

It even reached a point where life seemed unbearable. I tried to tell myself that it was all insane. If I didn't finish the doctoral dissertation, what I had already written would more than suffice for the comprehensives. Even if I didn't have the makings of a great philosopher, I still could become a decent schoolteacher. But rational arguments didn't help at all. I couldn't cross the street without hoping to be run over or go hiking without wanting to fall so that I wouldn't have to come back alive.

Nobody had the least idea of what was going on inside me. At the meetings of the philosophical society and at Reinach's seminars I always seemed happy—because I was working along with others. It was the end of these sessions—the only times when I felt secure—that I dreaded. Then the solitary struggle would begin all over again.[12]

A feeling of insecurity and abandonment gnawed at the normally self-confident student. Again, it was Reinach who helped her, encouraging her to go on with her thesis and responding sympathetically to the problems she was experiencing. During her visits to the Reinachs' home, Edith Stein was introduced to his wife and sister. Here, she was placed in the unfamiliar situation of having to look up to others rather than be admired by them. The Reinachs all handled intellectual projects with just the sureness her own approach lacked. Rather than generously bestowing advice and assistance on those in need, as she had been accustomed to do, at the Reinachs' she was forced to become aware of her own frightening limitations: "I didn't yet have the sort of intellectual clarity where the mind relaxes after it has gained some new insight, sees the vistas that have opened up before it, and then advances with confidence. I groped around like someone in a fog."[13]

12 Ibid., pp. 197–98.
13 Ibid., p. 201.

During World War I, Reinach and his wife were baptized as Lutherans. He wrote from the field that in future his role as a philosopher would be to bring others to faith. Other phenomenologists followed his lead. Edith Stein was not unmoved by these events. Though the pressure of studies kept the issue of faith temporarily in the background, she nonetheless sensed the beginnings of an interior transformation. "I couldn't undertake any systematic study of the problem of belief at that point—I was much too involved with other things for that. All I did was take in the stimuli the environment provided without resisting them. In consequence, I started to be transformed almost without my knowing it."[14]

Once initiated, this process progressed slowly but inexorably, despite the fact that most of her conscious attention was absorbed by the dissertation and preparations for her upcoming comprehensives. Her reason may have still shied away from reaching a definite decision about God; it could no longer simply deny the possibility of his existence.

As the draft began calling up many of her friends for service in World War I, Edith Stein, not wishing to be outdone in courage, volunteered together with numbers of other women students for duty in the military hospitals. She requested an assignment at the Hospital for Infectious Diseases at Mährisch-Weisskirchen. "My life isn't my own anymore [she wrote]. All my energy belongs to the great undertaking. When the war is over, if I'm still alive, then there'll be plenty of time to think about my own affairs again. . . . Naturally, I offered my services without restriction. If there was anything I wanted, it was to be sent out as soon and as far as possible, preferably to a field hospital on the front."[15]

Edith Stein devotedly cared for the soldiers of the Austrian army who were suffering from typhus, dysentery, and cholera. One of her friends and coworkers, Margarete Behrens,

[14] Ibid., p. 183.
[15] Ibid., p. 214.

described the spirit that supported them in their nursing work: "We were really so glad to be helping, relieving whatever suffering we could. The registered nurses under whom we served didn't make our job easy for us. Probably, they wanted to let us know that our "higher education" didn't mean a thing in comparison with their nursing training and experience. And of course they were right. But we didn't let that discourage us."[16]

Writing in her autobiography about some of the doctors whom they assisted, Edith Stein revealed the motives behind her decision to volunteer.

> There was only a single German doctor who worked with us, Dr. Scharf, a friendly Austrian. He did his job well; I always liked being assigned to help him. After he had finished up, he enjoyed sharing a couple of words with us. It wasn't long before he had found out what I did "as a civilian". (There seemed to be no point in keeping it a secret anymore.) Dr. Scharf wanted to know my reasons for interrupting my research to come here—the fact seemed to astonish practically everyone. I told him that since my fellow students were out in the field, I didn't see why I should have things better than they did. I think that impressed him.[17]

Edith Stein appears to have had a natural gift for forming friendships in every situation. Gentle, considerate, and self-possessed, she was always at the center of a large and ever-expanding circle of friends. Back at the university, her fellow students deeply appreciated her for her quiet, down-to-earth ways. One of them, Lilli Berg-Platau, described her as the most good-natured person she had ever known. As a result of the struggle with faith that Edith Stein was then undergoing, she grew to be even more modest and good-natured, as well as more aware of her limitations. "When I knew her, she was still very young, but even then she struck me as a person of fully mature character. There was something so modest and unas-

---

[16] Edith-Stein-Archiv, Karmel Köln.
[17] Stein, *Jüdische Familie,* p. 250.

suming about her. She never dominated a conversation or showed off with her accomplishments and great learning. . . . She was so careful to avoid giving the slightest impression of being superior."[18]

On completion of her term as a volunteer at the military hospital, Edith Stein was awarded the medal of valor in recognition of her selfless service. Working in a community gathered together by an accident of fate, in which death loomed as an ever-present threat, she learned that dedication and not knowledge is of ultimate importance. It is this that explains her subsequent change of attitude toward her studies. Even though she returned energetically to work once her job at the hospital was over,

> for all my commitment to studies, what I truly hoped for in my heart was a great love and a happy marriage. Somehow, without any knowledge of Catholic dogma or moral teaching, I had become imbued with the Catholic ideal of marriage. There was actually someone I met at the university whom I thought of as my future husband. But practically no one had any idea of this; to most people I seemed cold and unapproachable.[19]

[18] Edith-Stein-Archiv, Karmel Köln.
[19] Stein, *Jüdische Familie,* p. 154.

Edith Stein as Husserl's assistant

Chapter 4

Husserl's Assistant

When, in 1916, Husserl was offered a professorship at the University of Freiburg, he asked Edith Stein to accompany him as his graduate assistant, having learned to treasure her unobtrusive help. During her first summer there, she submitted her dissertation on "The Problem of Empathy" and was awarded the doctoral degree *summa cum laude*. That accomplished, she assumed responsibility for initiating the students in Husserl's proseminars into the new and unfamiliar area of phenomenology. She also spent a good deal of time reading and editing Husserl's shorthand manuscripts.

She received painful news toward the end of 1917: Adolf Reinach, friend to the young phenomenologists, had been killed on the battlefields of Flanders. Her heart went out to Frau Reinach in her loss. Yet when the family invited her to Göttingen to put the philosopher's papers in order, she hesitated. She felt disoriented by Reinach's death. He, after all, together with Husserl, had formed the nucleus of the Göttingen group; it had been his kindness that had allowed her to glimpse a world that was formerly sealed. Still without faith in life after death, these memories left her burdened. She wondered if she would find words to say to the grieving widow.

The resignation she encountered when she met Frau Reinach struck Edith Stein like a ray from that hidden world. Rather than appearing crushed by her suffering, the young widow was filled with a hope that offered the other mourners consolation and peace. Edith Stein's rational arguments crumbled in the face of this experience. Not the anticipated intellectual insight, but contact with the essence of truth itself transformed her. The light of faith broke in on her—in the mystery of the Cross. Although it would be years before she would live out the full consequences of this encounter—with her academic training, it would not be easy to abandon her carefully formed arguments for the sake of a leap into a new existence—so decisive was the influence of this experience that, shortly before her death, she was still talking about it to her Jesuit friend, Father Hirschmann: "It was my first encounter with the Cross and the divine power that it bestows on those who carry it. For the first time, I was seeing with my very eyes the Church, born from her Redeemer's sufferings, triumphant over the sting of death. That was the moment my unbelief collapsed and Christ shone forth—in the mystery of the Cross."[1]

Edith Stein began to read the New Testament, wondering whether she would eventually convert to Lutheranism or Catholicism. In either case, it was obvious that the new world burgeoning within her had dimensions unknown to scholarship and philosophical research. Formerly unnoticed "coincidences" of daily life suddenly took on the aspect of signs of God's loving providence:

> Because I had decided to study a particular subject, I had chosen the university that would take me farthest along in my field. . . . The fact that I got to know someone who "by coincidence" was also studying there, and that one day I happened "by coincidence" to discuss my philosophy of life with him—at first, I didn't notice any connection among all these things. But in retrospect, I now see clearly that this conversation exerted a decisive influence on me, more of an "essential" one, perhaps, than all the studying I did there, and I am struck

by the thought that it may have been "for that very reason" that I had to go live in that city.[2]

She also became aware of a change in her personal outlook: "I came to accept the fact that 'telling people the truth' usually doesn't improve them. In order for that to happen, people themselves have to want to improve and be open to accepting criticism from others."[3]

Edith Stein's religious struggle, which had received its initial impetus in Göttingen, grew more intense in Freiburg. This, in part, can be attributed to the fact that she served as Husserl's assistant there just at the time when Germany was undergoing the throes of military defeat. A spirit of pessimism and depression prevailed throughout the country; the suicide rate dramatically increased. One of these casualties was a friend of Edith Stein. Yet, despite the extreme darkness of the situation, her personal courage and spirit of affirmation enabled her to believe in the final victory of truth. As she wrote to her sister Erna:

> For the time being, I would ask you to look after Rose as much as you can. This is the worst thing that could have happened to her. There's no question that it makes quite a difference that it's suicide we're dealing with rather than a natural death. It makes it all the harder for us. But we'll have to try to accept this, too, and see if any good can come from it.
>
>   It really hurts me to hear such absolutely pessimistic statements coming from you and Rose. If only I could inject into you a little of the power that seems to flow into me after each new disaster. All I can say is, after everything I've gone through over the past year, I want to affirm the value of life more than ever. I'm enclosing an essay by Rathenau so you can

---

[2] Edith Stein, *Endliches und Ewiges Sein. Versuch eines Aufstiegs zum Sinn des Seins,* Edith Steins Werke, Bd. II (Louvain: Nauwelaerts/Freiburg: Herder, 1962), p. 109.

[3] Edith Stein, *Aus dem Leben einer jüdischen Familie. Kindheit und Jugend,* Edith Steins Werke, Bd. VII (Louvain: Nauwelaerts/Freiburg: Herder, 1965), p. 161.

see that there are other people who think about the outcome of
the war the same way I do. Sometimes, I really believe that we
have to get used to the idea that we may not survive the end of
the war. But that's no excuse to despair either. If only we didn't
limit our vision to the little bit of life in front of us, and then,
only to what's immediately visible on the surface.

If there's anything certain, it's that we stand at a turning
point in mankind's spiritual development—which means that
no one ought to complain if the crisis lasts a little bit longer than
he himself considers suitable. The horrors that we're now experiencing—and I'd be the last one to excuse them—are part of
the old spirit which remains to be overcome. But the new spirit
is present already, and I have no doubt that eventually it will
prevail. You can see it at work in philosophy and in the beginnings of a new kind of art in Expressionism. And just as surely
as materialism and naturalism have been ousted here, it is
equally certain that the same thing will happen in other areas of
life, though perhaps only slowly and after great struggle. The
same thrust can also be felt in the current political and social
struggles where the dominant concerns have become quite different from the old slogans people still hang on to. There's
good and evil, sense and nonsense on all sides here, though of
course nobody wants to see anything but the positive side of his
own position and the negative side of everyone else's (and that
goes just as much for nations as political parties!).

All of this has now been released into the atmosphere in a
whirl of tremendous confusion, and who can tell when peace
and tranquility can be expected again. Life is just far too complicated for anyone to figure it out with a brilliant world-
improvement plan that will let us know how things are going
to turn out in the future.

Please understand that none of the above is directed against
you personally. To a certain extent, I think we're in agreement.
I only wish I could get you to the point of believing that ultimately this process of change, which we scarcely saw coming
before it happened and now can do so little to control, is for the
best.[4]

---

[4] Edith Stein, *Selbstbildnis in Briefen* I. Teil 1916–1934, Edith Steins Werke,

Such was Edith Stein's sober estimate of the political situation at the end of the war. Trusting in the power of acceptance and patient waiting, she insisted that the realities of life could be endured, in spite of all the difficulties. But how could such a positive stance toward existence be kept up at a time like this? In the case of Edith Stein, the affirmation was nourished by a sense of "resting in God" that she occasionally experienced the closer she came to faith. An inner yearning had been enkindled through her encounter with Christ, which would later be described with the words, "My yearning for Christ was one continual prayer."[5]

This movement toward faith, however, was also a source of new suffering for her. Although she believed in God and in Christ, she could not bring herself to take the ultimate step of conversion. A number of difficult personal experiences, and the recognition that working with Husserl was no longer possible, made it a very painful period. This complex interior struggle reflected itself in her scholarly output. Though the papers from those years — "Psychic Causality", "The Individual and the Community", "An Examination of the State" — indicate a brilliant use of the phenomenological method in forming strict and penetrating analyses of experiences, states of awareness, and the structure of the soul, considered both from its material and spiritual aspects, what is really striking about them is that in every case the problem of faith arises in conjunction with a state of exhaustion brought about by a series of personal misfortunes. Under the guise of objective description, Edith Stein was depicting her own plight, her battle against "the shadow of death", and her own most intimate longing for "life". "I can want to believe with all my heart and work at it with all my strength, but that doesn't mean that my desire will necessarily be granted. Similarly, I can immerse

---

Bd. VIII (Druten: De Maas und Waler/Freiburg-Basel-Vienna: Herder, 1976), Letter 24, pp. 35–36.

[5] Posselt, *Edith Stein*, p. 55.

myself in the greatness of someone's character without being able to offer him the recognition he deserves."[6]

It took the agony of a "spiritual night" before Edith Stein could surrender to God. A period ensued in which her ordinary vigor and determination were cut off, depriving her of both the will and the ability to act. A "stillness of death" came over her, which prevented her from making an adequate response to God's call as mediated by the outside world. She described herself as being unable either to think or truly to love. All that sustained her at this time was an interiorly experienced "influx" of God, and even that remained imperceptible up to the moment of supreme exhaustion:

> There is a state of resting in God, an absolute break from all intellectual activity, when one forms no plans, makes no decisions and for the first time really ceases to act, when one simply hands over the future to God's will and "surrenders himself to fate". I myself have experienced this state to some extent. It came in the wake of an experience which had overtaxed my strength, drained my spiritual resources and robbed me of the ability to act. Compared to that inertia arising from a lack of vital energy, "resting in God" is something entirely new and distinct. One is a kind of "stillness of death", whereas the other is marked by a sense of tremendous security . . . which, to the degree I give myself to it, fills me with life. . . . This invigorating flow of energy appears to be the result of an activity other than my own.[7]

Yet until her mind was ready to be still, even an experience of human love did not relieve her. Her mind found new ways to resist God's attempt to reveal himself indirectly through the "phenomenon" of his reflecting image:

---

[6] Edith Stein, "Psychische Kausalität, Beiträge zur philosophischen Begründung der Psychologie und der Geisteswissenschaften", in *Jahrbuch für Philosophie und phänomenologische Forschung,* Bd. V (Halle: Niemeyer, 1922; reprint Tübingen, 1970), p. 43.

[7] Ibid., p. 76.

A convinced atheist learns through personal experience that there actually is a God. Now faith can no longer be eluded. Yet he can still refuse to ground himself in it or to let it become effective in him, choosing instead to hold on to the "scientific world view" that he knows an unmitigated faith would be the end of. . . . Or again, someone can offer me affection. There's no way I can stop him from doing it, but I don't have to respond to it. I can always pull myself away.[8]

How intense her interior struggle eventually became can be deduced from the following:

I can go ahead and make all sorts of plans—to take a trip over the coming year, for instance, or to move to another city or finish up some project I'm engaged in—and can even arrange my whole life on the basis of these plans. Deep down, however, I'm really convinced that something will happen to interfere with all my plans, and so I never have faith in any real or living way; my faith never has any effect on me.[9]

Edith Stein had undeniably been touched by God at the "core" of her personality, that immutable ground of the spiritual person which would remain the focus of all her philosophical investigations. And yet, "this inner sphere is not only beyond the reach of all external influences, it is also beyond all the attempts of the self to mold it. Therefore, when a change occurs within this sphere, it cannot be considered the result of some 'development', but a transformation accomplished by some transcendent power, a power outside the individual and the entire nexus of natural circumstances."[10]

In other words, though faith had opened up a new direction for her life and she had responded with an intellectual willingness to believe, it was not enough. God is a lover who requires the surrender of the will from those he loves to achieve his transformation. Apparently, this surrender was too frighten-

[8] Ibid., pp. 43–44.
[9] Ibid., p. 44.
[10] Ibid., p. 210.

ing for Edith Stein, as evidenced by the objections constantly raised by her intellect. Therefore she continued to "make plans"—in this case, to leave Freiburg and return to Göttingen to do the *Habilitation*.[11] Husserl composed a glowing recommendation for her, but his influence at the time was very limited. With the recent military defeat and the resultant political unrest uppermost in the minds of the Germans, circumstances were not conducive to hiring a woman professor, still something of a novelty in the years after World War I. Her application was rejected.

In 1919, Edith Stein went back to Breslau to continue with her research and await a change in the general situation. Her persistent interest in politics led to an active concern about current issues. The essays she wrote in 1920 about the individual and the community and about the state reveal the development of her thinking on these subjects. While discussing the reciprocal relations between individual and community, Edith Stein also examined the pertinent religious questions. Most important here was the restriction she placed on the state's competency in religious matters. Because the state cannot be the bearer of religious values, she argued, it cannot justifiably encroach on the individual's religious or personal existence. It is almost as if the events of the 1917 Russian Revolution gave her a premonition of the impending horrors the European atheistic dictatorships would cause. She concluded her researches by asserting the "inextinguishable uniqueness" of the human person, who lives at the same time in a state of spiritual "interconnectedness" with the rest of reality.

While working on these philosophical projects, Edith Stein also gave private lessons in phenomenology and continued the search for a definitive solution to her own religious questions. An experience she had on a visit to the cathedral in Frankfurt affected her deeply:

[11] A *Habilitation* is a second doctoral degree, done at the university where one will be teaching. —TRANS.

We went into the cathedral for a few moments, and as we stood there in respectful silence, a woman came in with her shopping basket and knelt down in one of the pews to say a short prayer. That was something completely new to me. In the synagogue, as in the Protestant churches I had visited, people only went in at the time of the service. But here was someone coming into the empty church in the middle of a day's work as if to talk with a friend. I have never been able to forget that. [12]

[12] Stein, *Jüdische Familie,* p. 282.

Chapter 5

Baptism

Along with her study of the Gospels, Edith Stein had also been reading the works of the Danish religious philosopher Sören Kierkegaard, particularly his *Training in Christianity*. But his emphasis on the individual standing alone before God, and his vision of faith as no more than a risk, a leap into the unknown, left her disappointed. Finally, in the summer of 1921, she arrived at the turning point that was destined to bring her long search for faith to an end.

Edith Stein was accustomed to spend long stretches of time visiting her friends the Conrad-Martiuses at their farm in Bergzabern.

> It was natural for her to come and stay with us for weeks at a time like all the other phenomenologists. We had the same friends that she did. . . . During Edith's last visit, we were both in the middle of a religious crisis. We stuck very close to each other like people walking along a narrow ridge, waiting for the divine summons to come at any moment. It did come, but ended up taking the two of us in two different directions.[1]

One evening, Edith Stein went through her friends' book-shelves looking for something to read. Her hosts had gone out; she was at home alone. The book she chose was the autobiographical *Life* of Teresa of Avila. Once she began reading it, she found it impossible to put the book down and stayed up

[1] Hedwig Conrad-Martius in *Edith Stein, Briefe an Hedwig Conrad-Martius* (Munich: Kösel-Verlag, 1960), pp. 65 and 72.

reading the entire night. When she finally finished it the next morning, she said to herself, "This is the truth."

What Edith Stein found in Teresa's autobiography was the confirmation of her own experience. God is not a God of knowledge, God is love. He does not reveal his mysteries to the deductive intelligence, but to the heart that surrenders itself to him. Along with being a mystic, Teresa of Avila was also a born psychologist and teacher of self-knowledge. Through her combination of mystical ardor and practical pedagogy, she succeeded in overcoming Edith Stein's "metaphysical prejudices" as well as her fear of encountering God. As Teresa asserted: "It is just the people who at first passionately embrace the world who penetrate farthest into the depths of the soul. Once God's powerful hand has freed them from its allurements, they are taken into their innermost selves."[2] Teresa's understanding of the soul went beyond "phenomena", "the active upper layer of the soul's life". For her, will, intellect, memory, and the essence of the soul were all undeniable objects of experience. As for "the most interior and personal part" of the soul, for Teresa who was no hypothetical entity scientists had posited in order to explain psychic data, but "something that could light up inside us and become actually perceptible, even if it always did remain mysterious".[3] Edith Stein discovered this "lighting" herself the night that she read the saint's life.

Edith Stein's experience with Teresa was no different from what had happened to Teresa herself four centuries earlier when reading Saint Augustine:

> Thanks be to God for giving me the life that rescued me from such an awful death. . . . After all the kindness I had received from you, my God, the hardness of my soul was almost

---

[2] Edith Stein, "Die Seelenburg", in *Welt und Person: Beitrag zum christlichen Wahrheitsstreben,* Edith Steins Werke, Bd. VI (Louvain: Nauwelaerts/Freiburg: Herder, 1962), p. 66.

[3] Ibid., p. 67.

unbelievable. I seem to have been almost totally powerless, as if bound by chains that were keeping me from making a total surrender to God. . . . Then I began to understand that I wasn't living but wrestling with the shadow of death. . . . My soul was utterly worn out; all it wanted was rest.[4]

It makes no difference what particular form this "shadow" assumes—sensuality as with Augustine, or worldly contacts as with Teresa, or attachment to a rationalist world view, as with Edith Stein. All that is necessary for a conversion to take place is that the individual honestly comes to recognize that his "death" is depriving him of the freedom to offer himself to God. Honesty and freedom, to Edith Stein, had always constituted the two greatest challenges imposed on the human person. Now she found them appearing with equal prominence in Saint Teresa.

According to Teresa, interior prayer is the setting where this inner resistance begins to be healed and transformed. Edith Stein wondered why she hadn't cultivated this silent inward prayer more seriously. Teresa's blunt explanation was, "If we refuse to let go of everything at once, we can't expect to receive the treasure of perfect love at once either."[5] Such a method evidently requires great courage, Teresa admitted, which is precisely why, "there are many people who have practiced interior prayer for a long time without ever reaching the goal . . . simply because they haven't embraced the Cross from the beginning."[6]

With Teresa, Edith Stein encountered the sign of the Cross for a second time. The Spanish mystic told her to let the intellect rest in prayer, to let God come to her in solitude and silence, without the props of earthly consolations:

At the time of prayer, we should allow the soul undisturbed rest and put all our knowledge off to the side. Scholars will

---

[4] Teresa von Avila, *Das Leben der heiligen Theresia von Jesus* (Munich: Kösel-Verlag, 1952), pp. 92, 93, 96, 97.

[5] Ibid., p. 107.

[6] Ibid., p. 113.

have plenty of time afterwards to serve the Lord with what they know. They will truly appreciate it then—so much so that nothing in the world will make them part with it, since they are using it in God's service where it really is quite helpful. But before God himself, believe me, a little training in humility . . . means more than all the learning in the world. Instead of establishing proofs and drawing conclusions, we will get to see ourselves honestly for what we are and to remain in simplicity before God. What he wants is for the soul to behave like a fool—which is just what it is in his presence. And he is so humble himself that despite all our wretchedness he's willing to keep us beside him.[7]

But Teresa also described the outcome of fidelity to this sort of prayer.

When God sees that the soul has been flying around for a long time like a bird, seeking him with the intellect, the will, and all the other faculties and doing its best to please him, then he rewards it even in this present life. And the reward is so tremendous that a single moment of it is enough to pay the soul for all of its earthly sufferings. . . . I was so blind! What ever made me think that I could find a remedy apart from you? Such stupidity—running away from the light.[8]

Fully aware that she was at the very beginning of the journey, Edith Stein nonetheless felt powerfully attracted by the vistas Saint Teresa revealed. She was ready to take on whatever difficulties the new life entailed, fortified by the saint's promise, "Once one has tasted a single drop of the water of this Kingdom, he is repelled by the taste of anything earthly. Imagine what it must be like to be completely immersed in it!"[9]

Edith Stein bought a catechism and a missal, studied them both thoroughly, and went to her first Mass in the parish

[7] Ibid., p. 145.
[8] Ibid., p. 166.
[9] Ibid., p. 198.

church of Bergzabern, celebrated by the pastor, Monsignor Breitling. Finding that she was able to follow the entire liturgy without difficulty, she went to the priest immediately after Mass and asked him to baptize her. The surprised Breitling informed her that normally a rather extended period of preparation was required. Rather than simply giving in, she asked him to examine her. This "examination" went so well that the monsignor set the coming New Year's Day as the date for administering the sacrament. From then on, attendance at the daily celebration of the Eucharist formed the center of her life.

On returning to Breslau, to all outward appearances life went on as before. She continued giving lessons and doing research, always trying to make herself available to her mother and her growing number of nieces and nephews. She wondered how she could best tell her family about her decision to become a Catholic. One person who aided her was Professor Günther Schulemann, university chaplain and vicar of the cathedral, a priest with whom she could discuss the question of conversion freely. Schulemann was impressed by Edith Stein's great modesty, aware of all the learning it kept concealed. Not being particularly inclined to phenomenology himself, he recommended reading Saint Thomas Aquinas as a preparation for entering the Church. His advice was accepted; gone were the days of being "obstinate and unteachable". In Schulemann's words: "Her great modesty was truly edifying. Already at that time she had the quiet and simple manner of a nun. Even my housekeeper of many years, who never let anyone's dark side pass unnoticed, used to say, 'What a sweet human being! You can't help being nice to her.' "[10]

Edith Stein's friendship with a young Jewish philosophy student to whom she gave private lessons in phenomenology provided another opportunity for discussing her hopes and difficulties. The student, later Professor Gertrud Koebner, has left behind a vivid account of their friendship which offers a

[10] Edith-Stein-Archiv, Karmel Köln.

number of insights into Edith Stein's religious development in the years prior to her conversion.

During the winter of 1918, Professor Julius Gutmann, the philosophy lecturer, advised me to familiarize myself with the phenomenological method. Although he felt a year studying with Husserl would have been the best thing, on account of personal reasons it was impossible for me to leave home at that point. As it happened, Professor Gutmann discovered that Edith Stein was just leaving Husserl to come back to Breslau. He approached her about the possibility of introducing me to the phenomenological method and tried to find ways of bringing us together. Edith Stein already had a widespread reputation in professional circles; as Professor Gutmann said, "If you're lucky enough to have her take you on, you won't find any better introduction to phenomenology."

Through Professor Gutmann's efforts I finally did get to meet Edith Stein at the home of a mutual friend. I was a little taken aback at first by her unprepossessing appearance and quiet manner, but as the conversation went on, the clarity and perceptiveness of her infrequent comments began to impress me. Since Edith Stein had a high regard for Professor Gutmann, his recommendation succeeded, and we agreed to get together for instruction on an informal basis. The plan was that twice a week I could come over to her home and "work".

We made good use of those hours at her desk. She was very serious about the work at hand and knew how to communicate the unfamiliar material in a patient, energetic, and unemotional way. Soon enough I realized what an outstanding teacher I had gotten hold of, and as she herself planned on remaining in Breslau and wanted to do a responsible job with our "classes", we switched our makeshift arrangement to a regularly organized schedule of meetings. Not long after that, she introduced the practice of ending each lesson with an invitation to tea. This is where I began to hear the stories that acquainted me with her many friends among the phenomenologists. I learned all about Husserl's colleagues as well as his students (particularly Edith Stein's dear friend Hedwig Conrad-Martius) and eventually came to feel completely at home in the Göttingen Circle without ever having met a single one of them. Her unparalleled gift for anecdote and characterization opened up a whole new world to me.

In the course of time—we stayed close up until the time she left for Speyer—she also showed me some of the letters which flowed in regularly from all directions, "goods received", as she called them. She had an interest in the scholarly research and personal concerns of her friends that astounded me. She was constantly occupied in "correcting" her friends' manuscripts as they arrived by mail; everyone wanted her opinion of their work while they were writing it.

I should also mention the special way she had of doing things. It was she, for instance, who taught me how to celebrate a birthday or a family get-together. For her, everything had a higher meaning: the most ordinary occasion would be transformed by the smile of heavenly joy it brought to her face. She was a person who found time for everything. Busy as she was, it was clear to her that she should live at home with her mother and actively join in the life of her large family. Her mother was the center of her life; being ready to care for her always took first place. Even though her suffering constantly increased as she thought about the break with her family her conversion would cause, somehow, the closeness she felt toward her mother seemed to grow along with it.

Sometime around the second year of our friendship Edith began reading the works of Saint Teresa, to offset Kierkegaard's *Training in Christianity,* which hadn't satisfied her. She read the books aloud over a period of time, more as if she were praying them than reading them. I remember how she often told me that these books contained something she had never been able to find in her own Jewish religion, even though she had seen it truly and faithfully practiced in her mother's home. Because of this, she said, she would have to live and act according to whatever she discovered in them, out of obedience to the Eternal Truth.

Edith's struggle began immediately after leaving Husserl. Though she yearned to dedicate herself totally to the truth, she could no longer believe that scientific truth, with which she was so thoroughly familiar, had the right to one's absolute devotion. For her the Eternal Truth shone on the Church, not the university. Nonetheless, she kept up her efforts to produce pure scientific work, always maintaining her scholar's appreciation for the value of scientific findings.

One day Edith showed me her missal, treasured as her most precious possession. I don't remember how she came to have it. Every Sunday, she translated portions of it for me at sight—with her, Latin was like German—and the devotion, reverence, and intense joy she showed as she read the prayers of Pope Gregory and drank in their spirit were totally indescribable. It was because the Lutheran Church had none of this that she could never become a Lutheran, even if her family might "forgive" the conversion more easily. And all this kept gradually progressing over the course of a number of years.

Hard as she tried to spare her mother pain, her mother understood this passionately loved child of hers better than Edith knew. I remember Edith telling me once that she always went to early Mass so that she could be home before anyone noticed it, and her mother telling me afterward with bitter tears that she had always heard the door close, no matter how quietly Edith left the house, and that she knew that it had to be Edith going off to church. But she never said a single word about it. Since I was at their home so frequently, her mother began taking me into her confidence and unburdening her heavy heart, especially in the later years, after Edith had moved to Speyer. Mother and daughter loved each other devotedly. Edith Stein wanted nothing more than to be a good daughter to her mother, and this remained true after she set out on her appointed path. On visits home, she would continue going to the temple with her mother just as before, making the long, tiring trip with her on foot since her mother wouldn't hear of riding on the holidays.

As we read Saint Teresa together, Edith revealed a little of her own interior life to me. You could see that it absorbed her utterly, that this was truly "home" for her. Yet she never distanced herself from her family or lost any of her immense affection for them. Even after she had fully decided on her future course and was only working out her method of procedure, she never let anything interfere with her love for her sisters and brothers and their children. It's impossible to imagine a more devoted nurse or babysitter than she. When she looked after the infants born during those years back home in Breslau, her face wore a smile from another world.

Bright as she was, she had to have known how her family would respond to her plans, though as it turned out, there were no recriminations on either side . . . simply a lot of suffering. Even her mother, who found it horrible to see her adored Edith becoming a Catholic, couldn't condemn it as a selfish act. There was too much love and humility in the way that Edith presented her decision.

Edith had a difficult road right from the start, between the pain she felt at causing her mother suffering and her joy at growing into her own authentic life. Later, as the abyss widened around her, she continued to feel secure in this inner existence. In fact, no matter how threatening the outward circumstances became, she only became freer and larger in spirit. Nothing was able to shake her confidence.

In consequence of our studies together, it eventually became clear to me that phenomenology was not the final goal, but only a method to help me supplement Kant's critical method rather than replace it. Though Edith had seen this development coming long before I did, she never dismissed my aesthetic difficulties, just as she never cut herself off from me after she entered Carmel. She was the kind of person who related to her friends with an openness and honesty that permitted them to see their life and work in clear perspective. She spoke only when she thought she could help, and then she was so candid that it made others candid in return. She was capable of uttering the most outspoken criticism, yet so totally devoid of condescension that it healed rather than hurt. As far as she herself was concerned, though, you always had the feeling that she was never satisfied with anything she had done. It wasn't enough for her to do a "passable" job; she wanted to devote herself completely and attain to the ultimate. When anyone came to discuss her problems she would bring up her own experiences and speak of them with such frankness that it made the meeting a unique event. Even though she may have had to go her own way alone, she wanted to provide help and com-

panionship to those who sought her out. Nothing was allowed
to stand in the way of this intention, neither social distinctions
nor any other obstacle. Only eternal values counted for
her. . . .

Edith knew that I would never abandon my Jewish faith and
scrupulously avoided any attempt to draw me away from it.
She knew that this was the one foundation on which our
friendship could endure.[11]

Edith Stein was baptized in Bergzabern on January 1, 1922,
taking the name "Teresa" as her baptismal name. It was an ec-
umenical event: her Lutheran friend, Hedwig Conrad-
Martius, stood as her godmother. A month later, on February
2, she was confirmed. Prior to conversion, she had always assumed that one day she would eventually marry. Now that
was no longer so. Together with faith had come the interior
call to consecrate herself to God by becoming a Carmelite nun.
Yet she knew it was not a decision she could carry out immediately.

Initially when I was baptized on New Year's Day 1922, I
thought of it as a preparation for entrance into the Order. But
a few months later, when I saw my mother for the first time after the baptism, I realized that she couldn't handle another blow
for the present. Not that it would have killed her—but I
couldn't have held myself responsible for the embitterment it
would have caused.[12]

Up to the moment she actually confronted her mother with
the news of her conversion, Edith Stein believed that she had
reckoned with the worst. But her mother's reaction caught her
unawares. "She wept. Edith Stein wasn't ready for that; she
had never seen her mother cry before. She had expected insults
and abuse and possible exclusion from the family."[13]

[11] Ibid.
[12] Teresia Renata Posselt, *Edith Stein. Eine Grosse Frau unseres Jahrhunderts,*
9th ed. (Freiburg-Basel-Vienna: Herder, 1963), p. 100.
[13] Ibid., p. 57.

Edith's brothers and sisters were shocked by her decision and puzzled by their mother's response. For them, Catholicism was a superstitious sect, known only through contact with the local folk customs. They imagined Edith "going around on her knees" and "kissing the shoes of the priest". Somehow their mother saw deeper. She sensed that her jealous wrath was out of place, that God, in his own unfathomable way, was placing his hand on her dearest child. As a family acquaintance wrote: "I'm convinced that what overpowered Frau Stein was the transformation she observed in Edith Stein that seemed to make a supernatural force radiate from her entire being. Being a God-fearing woman, she was able to feel, though not to comprehend, the holiness emanating from her daughter. For all her deadly anguish, she knew that she was powerless against the mystery of grace."[14]

Edith Stein continued to attend synagogue with her mother, where she surprised her by praying the Psalms of the synagogue service out of the Roman breviary. Deeply moved by her daughter's devotion, Frau Stein confessed, "Never have I seen anyone pray as Edith did."[15] It was this prayer that enabled Edith Stein to persevere against all opposition and to proclaim with Teresa of Avila:

> [I understood now] what it means for a soul to abide in truth in the presence of Truth itself. In this divine Truth I have come to know truths of the utmost importance—far better than if many scholars had explained them to me. . . . The truth that I said was communicated to me is Truth in itself, truth without beginning or end. From it there spring all other truths, just as all love springs from this Love and all glory from this Glory. And compared to the clarity with which the Lord revealed it all to me, what I have just said is obscure indeed.[16]

[14] Ibid.
[15] Ibid., p. 58.
[16] Teresa von Avila, *Leben*, p. 413.

Chapter 6

The Teacher

"Immediately before my conversion, and for a long time after, I thought leading a devout life meant giving up everything earthly and living only in contemplation of heavenly things."[1] After her baptism, Edith Stein gave up plans for a scholarly career and accepted a position teaching German at the Dominican sisters' school in Speyer. It didn't take long to settle into Saint Magdalena's, her sphere of activity for the next eight years. She appreciated the opportunity of sharing in the life of a religious community and easily adapted to the convent routine. Essentially, her life in Speyer was comprised of a balance between work and prayer. During this period, the search for God that had marked the years before her conversion increasingly grew into a discovery of him, both in herself and in the neighbors God entrusted to her. Though her role as a teacher consumed the bulk of her energy, frequently necessitating the sacrifice of her treasured times of private prayer, she learned to renounce these freely as the situation demanded.

Edith Stein regarded education as a form of apostolate and generously devoted herself to the needs of her students—the girls at the secondary school, the students at the Teacher Training Institute, the Dominican teacher candidates and novices. Their own testimonies bear this out: "She rapidly won

---

[1] Edith Stein, *Selbstbildnis in Briefen* I. Teil 1916–1934, Edith Steins Werke, Bd. VIII (Druten: De Maas und Waler/Freiburg-Basel-Vienna: Herder, 1976), Letter 45, p. 54.

her students' hearts, serving us all as a shining example with an influence that has lasted down to the present day. Modest and unassuming, she went about her work basically unseen and unheard, always equally friendly and ready to be of help."[2]

In this retired existence deliberately chosen as a means of growing in the interior life, Edith Stein learned to appreciate the demands and difficulties of the teaching profession. Her work in the narrow realm of the convent school prepared her for future responsibilities as a lecturer and a public speaker. A letter from this time indicates the manner in which she approached her new obligations:

> The most important thing is that teachers really possess the Spirit of Christ and embody it in a living way. But they also have the further responsibility of becoming familiar with the kind of life their students will have to face. Today's younger generation has gone through too many crises to be able to understand us anymore. So we're going to have to try and understand them, if we want to be able to offer them a little help.[3]

Edith Stein was a sympathetic and accommodating teacher who worked hard to convey her material in a clear and systematic manner. Yet her primary concern extended beyond the transmission of knowledge to include the formation of the whole person. As one student wrote:

> To be honest, she gave us everything. Though we were all very young at the time, none of us has ever been able to forget the spell that her personality exerted. Her manner alone made her a model for us at that critical age. There's not a single remark of hers that I can repeat—and it isn't that her comments weren't memorable, but that she was a quiet, untalkative person who could influence us simply by who she was. Whenever she had to offer criticism, she always did it with the perfect balance of

---

[2] Teresia Renata Posselt, *Edith Stein. Eine Grosse Frau unseres Jahrhunderts*, 9th ed. (Freiburg-Basel-Vienna: Herder, 1963), p. 59.

[3] Stein, *Briefe 1*, Letter 123, pp. 119–20.

fairness and kindness. Nobody ever saw her as anything but tranquil, dignified, and calm.[4]

Inside the classroom, Edith Stein displayed all the essential traits of a good educator. Her firmness and personal rectitude rapidly gained her the respect of her students; her gentleness won their confidence. Outside of school, she enjoyed going on walks with the students, sharing their jokes and listening to their problems. Many of them initially responded with an embarrassed awe at being with someone of her intellectual and spiritual stature:

> I had my first look at Fräulein Doctor Stein from the window of my classroom as she crossed the courtyard with a pile of books under her arm. Without having the faintest notion of who this person was, I was so impressed with her appearance that I can't forget it even today.
>
> In very few words—mostly by her personality and everything she did—she succeeded in setting the course not only for my studies but for all my future moral aspirations. With her you sensed you were in the presence of something pure, sublime, and noble, something that elevated you and brought you to its own level.[5]

Quickly enough, however, Edith Stein's students recognized that they had found a person who understood and cared for them. One of her pupils wrote of the sense of maternal warmth which she experienced:

> In my compositions, I felt able to express my personal opinions and my intimate feelings without any hesitation, knowing that only she would read them. I was convinced that I could say absolutely anything, be totally honest and open, without being misunderstood. I was going through many problems at the time, but most of them were easier to bear than losing her as a

---

[4] Posselt, *Edith Stein,* p. 61.
[5] Ibid., p. 63.

teacher, which is what eventually happened when I had to transfer to another school.[6]

In short, Edith Stein was more than just a teacher to her young students. She was a friend whose affection compensated for what many of them lacked at home, someone they knew would sympathize and share their problems. As regards her work with novices, Father Erich Przywara, the philosopher of religion, believed that her influence with them was comparable to that of a novice mistress. Przywara, who was introduced to Edith Stein in 1925, had frequent opportunity to observe her effectiveness firsthand. In his opinion, "Edith Stein was not only the finest educator the students at Saint Magdalena's had; thanks to a wise prioress, she was also a formative influence on the sisters and those starting out in religious life. The best members of that community owe their vocation to Edith Stein. To this day they remember the extent to which she actually functioned as their novice mistress."[7]

Lastly, in addition to the above, Edith Stein also supplied some much-needed assistance in the work of the teachers' college.

Astounding as it seems, Edith Stein went on to extend her activities to include the poor of the city. She looked on their needs as her first obligation, once she had met her professional requirements:

> God alone knows how many people she helped, counseled, and guided as an angel of mercy in spiritual and material crises. There were often many claims on her attention and an extensive correspondence to be maintained, yet she always found time to meet new requests. She once described her guiding principle as follows: "On the question of relating to our fellowmen—our neighbor's spiritual need transcends every com-

[6] Ibid.

[7] Erich Przywara, S.J., "Edith Stein", *In Und Gegen* (Nuremberg: Verlag Glock und Lutz, 1955), p. 24.

mandment. Everything else we do is a means to an end. But love is an end already, since God is love."[8]

Every year, in the busy weeks before Christmas, Edith Stein managed to prepare and deliver packages to the needy. Her room throughout December was a constant buzz of activity. Along with the gifts for the poor, there were numerous presents to be wrapped in holiday paper for all the friends she wanted to remember. Throughout the year, she would spend very sparingly on herself so as to be able to be generous at Christmas.

All this having been said, the most moving "sermon" the "Fräulein Doctor" preached during her years in Speyer was the long hours she spent in church. Because work left her so little time for prayer during the day, Edith Stein adopted the practice of praying at night, often spending whole nights by herself in the convent church. In the morning, she would go on to teach as if nothing extraordinary were happening. Yet it did not go unnoticed by her students: "It gave us some idea [one of them remembered] of what it means to bring faith and action into absolute harmony."[9]

Edith Stein did not allow her professional and charitable activities to keep her from remaining in close contact with her family. She went home to Breslau every summer, hoping to ease her mother's disappointment over her conversion. During these vacations, she often went to visit Professor Schulemann, occasionally taking along her sister Rosa, who, to her great joy, was also planning to enter the Catholic Church. As Schulemann recounted:

> Edith Stein came to tea every so often and once in a while she brought along her sister. She too impressed me at the time as being a person of genuine depth. In a way I think that she looked up to Edith, but she herself had a delightful personality

[8] Posselt, *Edith Stein,* p. 59.
[9] Ibid., p. 61.

In Speyer (1923)

all her own. Both of them possessed the marks of a tremendous self-discipline, as a result of the constant consideration they had had to show over the years for the customs and traditions practiced at home. They wanted at all costs to avoid alienating or offending their mother and even hoped eventually to win back her confidence.

Sometimes we discussed present-day Judaism:[10] the holiday customs, the long fasts (even in her eighties, their mother would not eat or drink at all during the whole Day of Atonement), and the traditional attitude toward death. Death—especially the death of one's parents—was regarded as something obscene, something with no right to exist. The very reference to the possibility of dying was treated as a terrible offense. When death actually did come, there was loud and unrestrained mourning, with no room given for consolation.

Once in a while, I ascertained purely by chance that Edith spent hours at a time praying in front of the tabernacle. Everything about her—her manner, her dress, her actions—was always refined, simple, dignified, and correct. During her vacations, she divided the day between prayer, study, and an affectionate participation in the life of her family. There were plenty of opportunities for conflict at home, but she always avoided them through her great patience and love. . . . Edith's position with the Dominicans, as well as the self-possession and serenity she displayed, gradually led her mother to suspect that Edith, as she put it, would probably add insult to injury and end up entering the convent.[11]

Such were Edith Stein's years in Speyer, an externally uneventful time, far removed from the mainstream of scholarship. She lived like a Dominican among Dominicans, pronouncing private vows and refusing to take any salary beyond what was necessary for clothing, room, and board.

[10] Edith Stein was then influenced by the Catholic doctrine on the Resurrection of Christ. She had no real experience of a more profound Judaism and the tradition of Judaism that people survive after death.

[11] Edith-Stein-Archiv, Karmel Köln.

Chapter 7

Thomas Aquinas

In 1925, Erich Przywara asked Edith Stein to translate some of the letters of Cardinal Newman. This was the beginning of a lively intellectual friendship between the two. Finding that she enjoyed the work, Edith Stein expressed an interest in taking on additional projects. It was providential that Przywara was there to rekindle her attraction to foundational research, this time within the context of faith. A thinker of her caliber needed deeper intellectual foundations for her belief. Echoing Professor Schulemann's advice, Przywara recommended translating Saint Thomas, still *terra incognita*[1] to the phenomenologist. The work he suggested was the *Quaestiones Disputatae de Veritate (Disputed Questions on Truth),* a key text in Thomas' thought as well as a sound introduction to the scholastic method. Once she began exploring Thomistic philosophy, Edith Stein not only strengthened her grasp of the doctrines of the faith, she also developed a new attitude to worldly activity: "I have gradually come to the realization that something more is asked of us in this world, and that even in the contemplative life, one may not sever the link with the world. . . . The deeper one is drawn into God, the more he needs to go out of himself—out into the world, that is, to carry the divine life into it."[2]

---

[1] *Terra incognita* means "unexplored territory".—Trans.

[2] Edith Stein, *Selbstbildnis in Briefen* I. Teil 1916–1934, Edith Steins Werke, Bd. VIII (Druten: De Maas und Waler/Freiburg-Basel-Vienna: Herder, 1976), Letter 45, p. 54.

Thomas proved to be the means of renewing her former commitment to philosophy: "The recognition that God can be served through scholarship first really struck me while studying Saint Thomas. It was only then that I could decide to take up scholarship seriously again."[3]

Edith Stein made her translation in half-hour periods stolen from her ordinary duties. It was not easy work. Philosopher though she was, she was a novice when it came to scholasticism, basically unacquainted with its fundamental terminology. Without her expert knowledge of Latin, she would never have dared to undertake the task. Yet she knew the translation was indispensable if she were ever to penetrate Thomistic thought.

Thomas' methodology presented the greatest obstacle for the phenomenologist. Her own natural bent being toward "direct investigation of phenomena", she found it hard to adapt herself to many of his unfamiliar concepts. Moreover, Thomas spontaneously employed arguments from both Greco-Roman and medieval Christian philosophy in his proofs, as well as texts from the Church Fathers and dogmas of faith. For Edith Stein, this was an unheard-of procedure. Just at an age where she might have been teaching philosophy herself, she found herself forced to submit her entire thinking to a process of reorientation. She accepted her role as a student—while continuing to retain the distinctive imprint of her phenomenological training. Soon she began to see the advantages Saint Thomas' comprehensive world view offered her over and above the purely epistemological insights of modern-day philosophy.

Thomas was both a philosopher and a theologian. As such, he was responsible for investigating angels, heaven, and God—hypothetical entities for the phenomenologist, yet eminently real to the believer. Hoping to make the medieval thinker as accessible as possible to the modern reader, Edith

[3] Ibid.

Stein converted his scholastic "disputations" into the more familiar form of the synthetic argument. She avoided the "distractions" of objections and counter-objections, and she limited her presentation to the discussion and solution of the problem under consideration. The remaining points were saved until the end of each question, where she treated them in a concluding commentary. Rather than seeking to produce an exact piece of philological scholarship, Edith Stein aimed at discovering the practical application of Thomas' insights. The philology she happily left to others. As she wrote in her foreword, "I would consider it especially gratifying if this translation had the effect of leading others back to the study of the original text."[4]

In the course of doing her translation, Edith Stein found that Aquinas' "hairsplittings", so often maligned over the centuries, deserved to be seen in a different light:

> Anyone who has spent some time in the company of this clear, penetrating, tranquil, and prudent intellect will frequently find that all of a sudden he can easily and definitively solve complex theoretical questions and practical problems that formerly had baffled him. If he reflects on how this possibly could have happened, he will discover, to his surprise, that it was Thomas with one of his little "hairsplittings" who laid the foundation for the solution.[5]

Though initially Edith Stein's motivation in translating Saint Thomas had been a practical one—to help herself and others conform their behavior to their faith—as she went on, she learned that faith has a further purpose: to serve as a path to truth. Notwithstanding modern philosophy's claim to an

[4] Edith Stein, *Des hl. Thomas von Aquino Untersuchungen über die Wahrheit (Quaestiones Disputatae de Veritate)* translation, Edith Steins Werke, Bd. III und IV (Louvain: Nauwelaerts/Freiburg: Herder, 1952), 1. Teil, p. 7.

[5] Edith Stein, "Husserls Phänomenologie und die Philosophie des hl. Thomas von Aquino", Supplementary Volume to *Jahrbuch für Philosophie und phänomenologische Forschung* (Halle: Verlag Niemeyer, 1929; reprint, Tübingen, 1974), p. 324.

all-inclusive grasp of truth, she discovered from Thomas that there are realms of truth from which philosophy must remain excluded apart from the enlightenment of faith. Faith, in fact, had given Thomas the courage to investigate the truth content of the natural reason and from there to trace the relation of formal and material dependence that reason had in relation to faith. Edith Stein uncovered many points of contemporary relevance in Thomas' epistemology, often establishing areas of substantial agreement between the saint's arguments and her own phenomenological findings. As the philosopher Peter Wust expressed it, her translation "presented to modern phenomenologists, still bound by subjectivism, the greatest phenomenologist of the objectivist Middle Ages as a clear mirror of their own ideas."[6] Through her patient efforts, phenomenology emerged as a fruitful medium for the expression of scholastic thought and at the same time gained a means of dialogue with the past.

Edith Stein's involvement with Saint Thomas advanced the process Teresa of Avila had begun in her. His crucial insights, far from being restricted to the relation between faith and reason, extended to the discussion of the mystical way. Even in the midst of his sober analyses, a sense of his personal experience of God breaks through: no one can speak as he does about faith, love, and the unity of the soul without having directly experienced God's love. Not without reason did Thomas call his lifework, the *Summa Theologica,* "a wisp of straw" in God's eyes.

While affirming the unity of the human person who thinks, contemplates, and loves, Thomas was drawn to assign a certain primacy to love. Faith, he stated, is the way to likeness to God, which is the goal of the human person; yet faith must always remain a dark way because the truths of faith cannot be grasped by the unaided workings of the human intellect. For

[6] Peter Wust, *Briefe an Freunde,* ed. W. Vernekohl (Münster: Regensberg Verlag, 1955), p. 97.

this they require divine illumination, and this in turn demands the cooperation of the will. What sets the will in motion is love. Contrary to the intellect, "The perfection of love does not consist in a certainty of knowledge but in an intensity of being seized."[7] Whereas faith, as "the substance of that which is hoped for",[8] aims at an object that is absent, love by its very nature is ordered toward the incomprehensible, to God, who himself is love. Thus,

> to the degree that the will is drawn to what is spiritual and divine, it moves farther away from the senses than the intellect does. The intellect is not capable of grasping its divine object to the same extent that the affections seek and love it. . . . Nor should it be maintained that the intellect achieves a greater proximity to its ultimate goal than the will. Even though it is by means of the intellect that the soul is drawn to God, it is the will which more perfectly attains to him.[9]

In other words, though faith is ordered to the contemplation of truth, it requires love to achieve its perfection. This is not to say that faith depends on philosophical demonstration; on the contrary, it bears its certainty within itself. In fact, as Thomas understood it, there could be no greater certainty than that of faith. This, however, did not prevent Aquinas from entering into extensive dialogue with non-Christian philosophers, where, rather than mixing philosophy and theology, he allowed reason to attain to its ultimate limits before introducing the standpoint of faith. He was not interested in forcing anyone to come to grips with the mysteries of faith; he was content to let the truth bear witness to itself.

Thomas' intellectual breadth had a liberating effect on Edith Stein. She expressed this influence in the essay she wrote for the *Festschrift* celebrating Husserl's seventieth birthday, "Husserl's Phenomenology and the Philosophy of Saint Thomas

---

[7] Stein, *Thomas von Aquino,* I. Teil, p. 268.

[8] Cf. Heb 11:1. —TRANS.

[9] Ibid., II. Teil, pp. 199–200.

Aquinas". In this paper written in dialogue form, after considering the points of methodological agreement between the two philosophers, she went on to speak of the fundamental intention both thinkers shared: "This is the way all genuine philosophers reach out to one another beyond the bounds of time and space, the way Plato, Aristotle, and Saint Augustine could be teachers for Saint Thomas (and this is worth emphasizing: Plato and Augustine, as well as Aristotle)—so much so that, apart from constant dialogue with them, philosophical reflection would not have been possible for him."[10]

Thomas did not use philosophy as a kind of stepping-stone to intellectual autonomy, priding himself on the supposed preeminence of his field. For him philosophy was simply one of the talents a person is given to help discover the mysteries of God within creation. This attitude led Edith Stein to develop a more objective stance toward the world. She recognized that her former absorption in prayer and renunciation of intellectual activity had been a means rather than an end. Once this was learned, separation from the world, though necessary at first, increasingly yielded to service of God. Her "natural productivity" as a philosopher had been restored.

[10] Stein, "Husserls Phänomenologie", p. 316.

Chapter 8

The Power of Prayer

Those who knew Edith Stein personally during the years in Speyer often remarked on her dedication to prayer. There were many who admired her for it, others who questioned its value. All of them wondered how she ever found time for an ongoing conversation with God in the midst of her exhausting teaching schedule, her work on the translation of Saint Thomas, and her active apostolate to the poor and the troubled. Perhaps it should be answered that it was the unfailing priority she offered to God that allowed her time for everything else.

> I don't use any extraordinary means to extend my working time; I just do whatever I can. Apparently, what I can do increases in proportion to the number of things that have to be done. When nothing urgent is called for, my energy gives out much faster. Heaven evidently has a sense of economy. . . . It all depends on having a quiet little corner where you can talk with God on a daily basis as if nothing else existed . . . and regarding yourself completely as an instrument, so that you treat your most frequently demanded talents, not as something that you use, but as God working through you.[1]

Rather than serving as a form of self-gratification, Edith Stein's prayer was the energizing force behind her professional work and her numerous charitable activities.

[1] Edith Stein, *Selbstbildnis in Briefen* I. Teil 1916–1934, Edith Steins Werke, Bd. VIII (Druten: De Maas und Waler/Freiburg-Basel-Vienna: Herder, 1976), Letter 69, p. 71; Letter 45, p. 55.

In the autumn of 1927, Edith Stein's spiritual director, Canon Schwind, died of a stroke while hearing confessions in the cathedral. The loss went deep: for the last five years the Schwinds had "adopted" Edith as a member of their family. Anna, the vicar's niece, loved to relate the following anecdote: "One day my uncle rushed into the kitchen, wringing his hands in dismay. Sinking into a chair, he exclaimed, 'That lady-philosopher! Ten theologians couldn't answer all the questions she asks me.' "[2]

In appreciation of the friendship and advice the canon had given her, Edith Stein composed an obituary notice for the Innsbruck clergy circular. Speaking of him in his capacity as director, she wrote:

> His method of spiritual direction was calm, firm, and prudent. Though he had broad human experience and decades of pastoral work to rely on, he always maintained a devout reverence for the workings of God in the soul. Consequently, he was able to be just as gentle as he was challenging. To anyone responsive to the leadings of the Spirit, he demonstrated a boundless confidence, allowing him to proceed without any interference. . . . He had an unshakable trust in the ways of divine providence and in the power of prayer, yet he could admonish when necessary, and it was this that enabled him to bring comfort and peace to situations where human consolation proved useless. . . . Severe and kind, serious and lighthearted, proud and humble—in him these opposing characteristics had grown into a unity, springing from the purest love of God.[3]

The following year, Father Przywara recommended that she attend the Holy Week liturgy at the Benedictine abbey of Beuron. By taking his suggestion, Edith Stein entered on a

[2] *Kölner Selig- und Heiligsprechungsprozess der Dienerin Gottes Sr. Teresia Benedicta a Cruce—Edith Stein,* eds. Teresia Renata Posselt, O.C.D., and Teresia Margareta Drügemöller, O.C.D. (Cologne, 1962), p. 85.

[3] Teresia Renata Posselt, *Edith Stein. Eine Grosse Frau unseres Jahrhunderts,* 9th ed. (Freiburg-Basel-Vienna: Herder, 1963), p. 69.

further phase in her spiritual journey. Here she met her new director, Dom Raphael Walzer, the monastery's young, dynamic abbot. Placing her concerns before him with her customary candor, she astounded the abbot by her simple, uncomplicated piety. As he wrote:

> By the time Edith Stein made her first visit to Beuron, she wasn't a spiritual novice anymore. She had brought such an inner richness along with her that, right from the start, she was at home in the monastic setting of this secluded little spot along the Danube. She certainly didn't need to undergo a transformation or learn anything essentially new. It was, on the contrary, the season for harvesting what others had sown in her already, what she herself had tended in such precious soil.[4]

Retreats at Beuron gave Edith Stein the opportunity to satisfy her thirst for prayer. Undisturbed, she would remain for hours on end, kneeling inside the abbey church. She regarded the privilege of attending the Holy Week and Easter Services as one of the great high points of the year.

Often she was noticed praying before a picture of the *mater dolorosa*.[5] "As I look back today," one woman commented, "I don't think Edith Stein was simply praying to be allowed to suffer. I think she somehow knew that one day she would actually take the path of suffering."[6]

At Beuron, Edith Stein's capacity for intense interior prayer received a healthy balance through exposure to the Benedictine public liturgical praise of God. Sister Plazida, O.S.B., has preserved the following story:

> On one occasion I was sent as a young religious to attend to community business near Speyer and was thus able to spend some time with Edith Stein over the weekend. She was just then in the middle of translating Saint Thomas' *Quaestiones Disputatae de Veritate*. She worked on this demanding project in

[4] Raphael Walzer, Edith-Stein-Archiv, Karmel Köln.
[5] This title of the Virgin Mary means "Mother of Sorrows". —TRANS.
[6] Posselt, *Edith Stein,* p. 74.

little bits of time snatched from her ordinary duties, yet always found time to conclude each day by reflecting on the appropriate portion of the Rule of Saint Benedict.

That Sunday morning we attended solemn high Mass in the cathedral together. For almost the entire liturgy, Edith Stein remained on her knees with her eyes closed and her face resting in her hands. To a young, liturgically minded Benedictine like myself, that made no sense at all. Afterward, I told her that at such a solemn Mass, you had to pray with your eyes and your ears. I don't remember what she answered, but I know that it made me very happy when I found out about her close association with Beuron. Not that I was surprised to hear that she eventually entered a Carmelite convent instead of a Benedictine monastery. But without the encounter with the Benedictine liturgical spirit at Beuron to release and develop her hidden interior resources, she would never have attained to the marvelous largeness and breadth of personality that were her hallmark.[7]

Grateful as she was to enter into the monastic liturgical tradition, Edith Stein never wavered in her initial attraction to Carmel. Her friend Countess Bissinger remembered, "Though Edith Stein was deeply attached to Beuron, her most profound love was always reserved for Carmel. You could see the happiness it gave her whenever she found someone who appreciated this attraction."[8]

In examining the motivation that drew Edith Stein so powerfully to prayer, Abbot Walzer wrote:

All that she wanted was to be with God in church and to have the great mysteries right in front of her. This was something her retreatant's cell could not offer her, nor the world of nature that lay just beyond the seclusion of the holy place. I'm convinced that in her time of prayer and meditation she didn't depend on many Scripture texts or do any biblical exegesis or prepare for all the lectures she was always being asked to

[7] Edith-Stein-Archiv, Karmel Köln.
[8] Ibid.

deliver. . . . The almost rigid exterior she presented while praying was matched by the interior quiet of a soul enjoying the blessed contemplation of God. Happy to be a convert who had come home to her mother the Church, she joined with the monks—the great Church at prayer—in proclaiming their common faith. She took Christ's admonition to "pray constantly" completely literally, so no liturgy was ever too long for her. . . . But it wasn't the austere beauty of the liturgy that most strongly affected her mind and heart. Though form certainly occupied a privileged position for her, as evident from her words, her appearance, and her actions, nothing human could distract her—neither the somewhat unfortunate aspects of the abbey church nor any of the other artistic imperfections that couldn't have escaped a person of her universal culture. She never let a one-sided aestheticism interfere with her reflection and prayer.[9]

Abbot Walzer did not support Edith Stein's wish to enter Carmel. Like many others, he was convinced that the Church had work for her to do outside the cloister. In the very years that Edith Stein was seeking out Beuron as a place of solitude and silence, invitations were regularly arriving, from abroad as well as at home, asking her to speak on the problems of contemporary woman. Obedient to the voice of the Church, Edith Stein renounced her personal desires. From this self-transcendence emerged a new sense of interior freedom and contentment. Abbot Walzer recalled, "I liked to apply to her the words the monastic breviary uses to describe the peace of a sanctified soul: *Fuit et quietus.*[10] Yes, she had that tranquility."[11] Little may be known of the inner dimension of Edith Stein's life of prayer, but there are a wealth of similar instances that testify to the quality of her everyday behavior.

[9] Ibid.

[10] This phrase, meaning "and he was quiet", is taken from the hymn "Iste Confessor". —TRANS.

[11] Ibid.

Often it was ordinary people who seemed to appreciate most readily her self-forgetful love of neighbor. Brother Anton Maunz, then porter at Beuron Abbey, has left behind these reminiscences:

> I got to know Fräulein Stein in Beuron, where I worked as a porter from 1922–1939. I spoke with her whenever she came to visit her spiritual director, Reverend Father Abbot Walzer, or any of the other monks. Fräulein Stein was modesty itself—the way she spoke, acted, dressed, and did her hair. When I found out that the visitor of the Lord Abbot's was really a very educated lady, I had to admire the way she spoke with me at the porter's lodge. I was also impressed by the reverence she showed for all the monks, even for ordinary lay-brothers like myself. She respected all of us religious as if we were "God-knows-what". Another thing that struck me was the patience she showed whenever there was a crowd or a long wait. Even though she probably had time to spare, I'm sure that once in a while she would have appreciated it if someone had taken care of her right away. But I never remember her insisting on having to be first or claiming special treatment because she had come to see Reverend Father Abbot. Every time I met her, she was just a plain, unassuming visitor.
>
> I was equally touched by the gratitude she showed for every little errand or favor that I did for her. Later on in Carmel, she still hadn't forgotten them and sent back holy cards of her Clothing on April 15, 1934, with a little handwritten message on the back for me and the sacristan, the late Brother Willigis Dirr. This was her way of expressing once again the undying gratitude she felt toward Brother Willigis and myself. She hoped they would give us a little pleasure—and of course they did. I still have them today and treasure them more than when I first received them. In her humility, she asked us to pray for her in the new life she was beginning. Someone in her position could have taken a very different attitude, but she purposely avoided making any selfish demands or trying to draw attention to herself. She wanted to be treated like everybody else, as a visitor in need of spiritual assistance. Brother Willigis felt the exact same way. She truly was a model human being.

There were some people that used to be scandalized at her habit of sitting in the front of the church. But she certainly didn't do it to make herself seen or because she thought she was somebody special. Brother Willigis and I always believed that the only reason she did it was so that she could participate in the liturgy better, without any distractions. She would always set out early for church, walking along quietly and reflectively. Some of these other "pious souls" dawdled up to the very last minute—or even longer—chatting with one another outside the church. Then, when they finally did come in, well, there was Fräulein Edith again, right in the front pews! Maybe there were other "shocking cases" like this, though I don't remember any. [12]

Actually, according to Abbot Walzer, nothing could have been farther from Edith Stein's mind than the desire to publicly parade her piety. "The only signs that ever gave any outward indication of the depth of her interior life were the balance between her gifts of mind and heart, her earnest approach to the problems of our age and her heartfelt compassion. [13] Her taxing intellectual labors had not diminished her feminine side in the slightest. She possessed, the abbot claimed, "a tender, even maternal, solicitude for others. She was plain and direct with ordinary people, learned with the scholars, a fellow-seeker with those searching for the truth. I could almost say she was a sinner with sinners." [14] The words of a friend confirm this total identification with the joys and sufferings of her brothers and sisters: "When it came to others, she showed tremendous gentleness. The more wretched a person was, the more pleasure she felt in seeking him out as one of God's favorites—just in the situations where the rest of us saw only misery and nothing more." [15]

[12] Ibid.
[13] Ibid.
[14] Ibid.
[15] Ibid.

Chapter 9

Addressing the Professional Woman

Edith Stein's first seven years in Speyer proved to be a preparation for greater tasks. Her philosophical writings and translations, far from going unnoticed, had attracted the attention of the Association of Catholic Women Teachers and the Association of Catholic University Graduates. The members of these organizations were eager to hear her express her views on contemporary issues. Beginning in 1927, Father Przywara assumed responsibility for setting up regular lecture tours. This brought the period of seclusion to an end. So overwhelming was the response to her lectures, both at home and abroad, that she was frequently forced to interrupt her teaching duties in order to take on engagements in Ludwigshafen, Heidelberg, Zurich, Salzburg, and the industrial region of the Rhineland. She began to wonder if it might not be her vocation to speak on "Woman's Significance in Contemporary Life".

Typical of her approach is the introduction to a speech she delivered in Ludwigshafen:

> Allow me to begin on a personal note. Two days ago, I traveled from Beuron, where I had the privilege of spending Holy Week and Easter, to Ludwigshafen, right into the middle of preparations for this conference. You can hardly imagine a greater contrast: Beuron, that quiet valley of peace, where day after day and year after year, the praise of the Lord is sung, undisturbed by outward events — and this assembly, which has come

together to discuss the most urgent issues of our time. It was almost like plunging from heaven to earth. And yet, the very contrast could be the symbol of the task which we have here before us.[1]

Edith Stein's forceful manner of presentation captivated her listeners. For years, these women had been searching for someone who would go beyond the sociological, psychological, and philosophical explanation of their basic questions about woman's identity to offer them an answer grounded in the power of faith. Many of them saw her as the embodiment of the answer she was attempting to formulate. As one schoolteacher wrote:

I was expecting to hear an imposing, self-confident, female Jewish intellectual, like so many of the ones I had encountered through the liberal women's movement and various charitable organizations—and a fascinating speech of course. But instead of an imposing personality all set to captivate you with her method of presentation and her intellectual brilliance, there appeared a small, delicate, surprisingly unpretentious woman, simply and tastefully dressed, who clearly had no intention of impressing you by her demeanor and her dazzling wit. In fact, there was almost something childlike in the way she introduced herself. Yet within her penetrating eyes lay something mysterious and solemn, and the contrast between this and her simplicity created a certain awe—at least in me.

She spoke unrhetorically, with quiet charm, using clear, attractive, unpretentious words. Despite this, you immediately sensed a tremendous strength of intellect and an extremely rich, intensely disciplined interior life springing from absolute conviction. . . . She neither accused, disputed, nor threatened. She simply stated the facts, and, in the course of her presentation, the dangers facing our nation became startlingly clear.

[1] Edith Stein, *Die Frau. Ihre Aufgabe nach Natur und Gnade. Beiträge zur Mädchen- und Frauenbildung 1922–1932*, Edith Steins Werke, Bd. V (Louvain: Nauwelaerts/Freiburg: Herder, 1959), p. 205.

. . . Then she called out, "The nation . . . doesn't simply need what we have. It needs what we are."[2]

Moved by her personal warmth and her sound approach, Edith Stein's audiences found themselves responsive to her message. For many of them, according to Father Przywara—clergy and laymen as well as women—her talks provided the first opportunity to come to a genuine appreciation of women's role.[3] She delivered her lectures in the years of trial and reconstruction coming between the end of World War I and the Nazi takeover. A look at their titles indicates the issues they treated. "The Ethos of Woman's Vocation", "The Vocation of Man and Woman in the Order of Nature and Grace", "The Life of the Christian Woman", "Foundations of Women's Education", "The Place of Women in Guiding the Young to the Church"—taken together, they form an outline of the central idea she wished to develop: woman's mature Christian life as a source of healing for the world.

Edith Stein began by delineating the effects of the shift from the individualism of the nineteenth century to the social orientation of the twentieth. She herself had experienced firsthand the consequences of this upheaval, so profoundly disruptive to the political and social order. Europe, she asserted, had emerged fundamentally altered from the catastrophic war of 1914–1918. In the aftermath of the conflict a new struggle had arisen between materialism and totalitarianism. Advancing technology had shrunk the dimensions of the globe, binding the nations of the world together for better or for worse. The distinction between public and private responsibility had blurred to such an extent that no longer could the plight of other nations be viewed without a sense of fraternal obligation. It was a time of universal economic and political adver-

[2] Maria Wilkens, "Erinnerungen an Edith Stein", in *Katholische Frauenbildung* 63. Jg. 1962, Heft 12, pp. 841–42.

[3] Erich Przywara, S.J., "Edith Stein", *In Und Gegen* (Nuremberg: Verlag Glock und Lutz, 1955), p. 64.

sity. Yet precisely because of these problems, it was the moment for women to reevaluate their role.

> After the life and death struggle of a World War, the nations of Europe have collapsed alongside one another, having learned through the bitter lessons of adversity that only a common effort can make recovery possible. Whether a policy of international conciliation will gradually prevail against strong counter-currents is impossible to predict with certainty. But one thing is clear: the issue involves women. If a woman's vocation is the protection of life and the preservation of the family, she cannot remain indifferent as to whether or not governments and nations assume forms which are favorable to the growth of the family and the well-being of the young.[4]

During the postwar years, women's sphere of activity had rapidly expanded from the home to the world. New opportunities had naturally led to new responsibilities. Edith Stein wondered how these obligations could be met without at the same time imperiling women's essential character. She knew that in the minds of many, traditionally male professions—medicine, teaching, engineering, and law—automatically constituted a danger for women. Women, as they saw it, had been created to help, nurture, and protect rather than to exercise a given technical competence. They predicted that, inevitably, professional life would stunt or fragment women's potential. Sensitive to these dangers herself, Edith Stein called for a full rethinking of the issue. She agreed that financial considerations were not sufficient reason for a woman to enter professional life. Work did generate certain tensions, and marriage did not guarantee an exemption from them. Professional life often profoundly affected the character of married life, exposing a wife to problems much like those of her unmarried counterpart.

[4] Edith Stein, *Frauenbildung und Frauenberufe,* collection of articles written after 1930, 4th ed. (Munich: Verlag Schnell und Steiner, 1956), p. 13.

Edith Stein believed that the solution of these difficulties lay in the development of a more adequate concept of the human person, and she formulated a model that unconsciously reflected the breadth of her own personality. Dispensing with available psychological and anthropological findings, she transferred the question of woman's vocation from its areligious context to one that presented both man and woman in their mutual complementarity and their individual responsibility before God. No longer was it possible, she argued, to restrict a woman's place to house and cloister. The fact was, women had come to function in the professional world as men's equals. Hence the traditional designation of the woman as wife and mother would have to be abandoned. Edith Stein supported her view with quotations from the New Testament, which, in recognizing a vocation to celibacy, implicitly acknowledged a significance for woman independent of man. Before God, according to the Scriptures, women have a unique and inalienable value of their own.

While not unsympathetic to the problems of those whose religious and moral foothold had been weakened by entry into professional life, Edith Stein was convinced that spiritual and intellectual reflection could enable women to face the challenges of the professional world. In the early Church, Christians had been driven to resist actively the ancient paganism for the sake of their new religion; today, Christians were being summoned to take part in the struggle against modern atheism, with its open advocacy of godlessness and its all-out attack on the principles of the Christian West. "More than anything else today, what is needed is the baptism of spirit and fire. This alone can prepare those who shape human life to take their rightful place at the front lines in the great battle between Christ and Lucifer. There is no more urgent task than to be constantly armed and ready for this battle. For, 'if the salt loses its savor, how can it be restored?' "[5]

5 Edith Stein, "Notzeit und Bildung", 1932 speech delivered in Essen.

Genuine preparation for the expanding role of women demanded training in affective values. Edith Stein looked to a balanced primary and secondary school curriculum to provide the groundwork for such formation. She discussed various possibilities for the reform of the exclusively male and intellectually oriented educational system and argued for a holistic approach in developing woman's potential. Pedagogy had to take into account the natural predisposition of women for the concrete and the particular, for the human being "in the flesh" as opposed to the abstract. It was crucial, she stated, that women be given the necessary resources for defending their specifically feminine individuality against forces that might otherwise distort or destroy it. For women were not meant to resemble men in all respects. Their helping and mediating role, rather than representing a diminished degree of personal freedom and independence, was the proper expression of God's design, fully compatible with their psychological and physiological make-up. A man might be ordained by nature to realize his cultural achievements primarily through the concentrated development of specific capacities; but a woman who entered the professions had another task: "to merge her vocation as a woman with her particular vocation and impress the latter with a feminine character."[6] Herein lay the ultimate solution to the problem, according to Edith Stein. Instead of simply functioning as a lawyer, doctor, teacher, or civil servant, a woman would always have the opportunity and the obligation to serve as a motherly companion for those with whom she worked. She would never be satisfied with applying a limited technical expertise; her actions would be the outflow of her own unselfish love.

Hoping to encourage her audiences in this direction, Edith Stein reflected on her own experience:

> Whether your contact with people comes through providing medical care, giving financial support, or offering legal assistance, the possibility (or more fundamentally, the necessity)

[6] Stein, *Die Frau,* p. 86.

always exists for involving and affecting the whole person. . . . This will impose an even greater burden on the capacity to love than a family does. Here, the natural ties are missing, the number of people is much greater, and, for the most part, they are men and women whose situation and current state of mind will tend to make them repulsive instead of attractive.[7]

Edith Stein was fully aware that sustaining this sort of commitment required more than human support. In "Paths to Interior Silence", an article written for the Societas Religiosa, an association of professional women, she described some practices that could assist in enlarging woman's spirit: prayer and interior silence. Women, she wrote, ought to become "broad", "tranquil", "emptied of self", "warm and transparent". Only hearts that are emptied and silent can be penetrated by grace, with its power to form women into the loving persons they are intended to be. Before they can be ready to assist others, women first need to be securely anchored in their own depths.

To foster this process, Edith Stein recommended living each day in a spirit of recollection and prayerfulness. Every woman, in the way most suitable to her, should try to find "breathing spaces"—moments in which she can return to herself and rest in God.

God is there [in these moments] and can give us in a single instant exactly what we need. Then the rest of the day can take its course, under the same effort and strain, perhaps, but in peace. And when night comes, and you look back over the day and see how fragmentary everything has been, and how much you planned that has gone undone, and all the reasons you have to be embarrassed and ashamed: just take everything exactly as it is, put it in God's hands and leave it with him. Then you will be able to rest in him—really rest—and start the next day as a new life.[8]

[7] Ibid., p. 71.
[8] Edith Stein, *Wege zur inneren Stille,* collected articles, ed. W. Herbstrith (Frankfurt: Kaffke Verlag, 1978), p. 48.

One concluding note: the "motherliness" that figures so prominently in Edith Stein's concept of woman should not be taken as a term of sentimental appeal. In her thinking, it was akin to the qualities of warm-heartedness and dependability. She herself said, "Because the need for motherly sympathy and help is universal, we can use this word 'motherliness' to sum up everything we have developed about woman's particular importance. But it should never be the kind of motherliness that remains caught in a little circle of family and friends."[9]

[9] Stein, *Die Frau,* p. 217.

Chapter 10

A Lectureship in Münster

The years 1930 to 1933 were busy ones for Edith Stein, filled with a variety of plans. Many of them centered around a short-lived teaching appointment that would simultaneously mark the culmination and conclusion of her scholarly career. In 1930, at the beginning of this period, her friends, heartened by the success of her lectures and the work she had done in translating Saint Thomas and introducing him to phenomenological circles, recommended that she reapply for a university professorship. A letter from December of that year alludes to the impression their suggestion made.

> For quite some time, I've been aware that I've never even an-swered your name-day greetings. I'm sure you can imagine why—the astonishing repercussions of my trip to Salzburg. Since then, I've been forced to make speaking appearances all over—with tons of papers to correct in between.
>
> At the moment, it looks as if I'll be leaving the school at Eas-ter (please don't say anything about this for the time being)— though I still don't know what will happen after that. Up until Christmas, I had put off thinking about it as just a useless waste of time, but now I plan to examine the entire question thoroughly at Beuron.[1]

Edith Stein left Saint Magdalena's in March 1931 in order to devote herself full time to writing. Hard as it was to say good-

[1] Edith Stein, *Selbstbildnis in Briefen* I. Teil 1916–1934, Edith Steins Werke, Bd. VIII (Druten: De Maas und Waler/Freiburg-Basel-Vienna: Herder, 1976), Letter 74, p. 75.

bye to both students and sisters, she knew that it was necessary. "I left Speyer on March twenty-seventh. Saint Thomas refuses to accept bits of stolen time any longer; he insists on having my undivided attention."[2] Here she was referring to *Act and Potency,* the consideration of the relationship between phenomenology and scholasticism which she was planning to submit to the universities as her *Habilitationsschrift.*[3] Already in the final weeks in Speyer she had begun to draw up the first draft.

Most of 1931 was spent in unsuccessfully applying to the universities of Freiburg and Breslau. Though she obtained interviews at Freiburg with Professors Finke, Honecker, and Heidegger, and Professor Koch actively campaigned for her in Breslau, it was all to no avail. The situation of the early post-war years was repeating itself, this time with anti-Semitism at work behind the scenes to obstruct the appointment. Edith Stein accepted the situation calmly, unperturbed by the cycle of hopes and disappointments that it involved. As she wrote to her old friend Sister Adelgundis Jaegerschmid, "You should try to explain to Professor Finke that interiorly the matter doesn't affect me. I will be neither sad nor disappointed if nothing comes of it."[4] Nonetheless, she had sacrificed a great deal to satisfy the universities' requirements: "I knew when I decided to leave Speyer that living outside a religious house would be very hard for me. But I had no idea that it would be as hard as it has been over the last few months. Still and all, I have not regretted it for an instant; I'm convinced that everything is exactly as it should be."[5]

Edith Stein moved back to Breslau—not only for the sake of her mother, who had finally accepted the idea of her daughter's holding a Catholic chair at the university, but also for

---

[2] Ibid., Letter 87, p. 85.

[3] This is the term for the dissertation written for the *Habilitation* referred to in chapter 4. — TRANS.

[4] Ibid., Letter 83, p. 82.

[5] Ibid., Letter 95, p. 92.

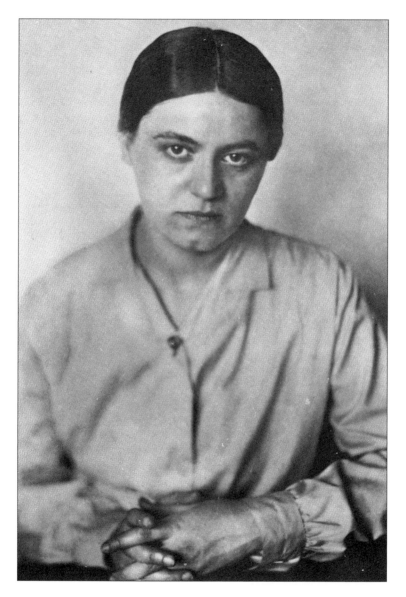

In Vienna (1931)

Rosa, badly in need of her sister's presence. Rosa, who had grown to feel increasingly alone and abandoned in her non-Christian environment, could not even consider an official conversion to Catholicism due to her mother's opposition. During Edith Stein's months back in Breslau, the two sisters often went to visit Professor Schulemann. For the most part, they avoided the subject of the *Habilitation,* knowing that the priest had little influence in academic matters. Schulemann's own view of the question can be found in his reminiscences, in which he asserts that a thinker of Edith Stein's caliber deserved better treatment, anti-Semitic prejudices and a neo-Kantian bias against phenomenology notwithstanding:

> Though Edith Stein and I hardly ever spoke of the *Habilitation,*
> I think it must be assumed that for a while, university teaching,
> especially in her native Breslau, presented itself as the fulfill-
> ment of a lifelong ambition. When someone's life has been as
> well-grounded intellectually as hers and developed with so
> much diligence, it has to have come as a tremendous shock not
> to have attained the anticipated goal, with all its opportunities
> for further advancement. This shouldn't be taken as a sign of
> pride or arrogance. There's not the slightest doubt that she had
> all the scholarly qualifications.[6]

While waiting for the universities' final decisions, Edith Stein continued to give lectures and to work on the revision of her translation of Saint Thomas, published in two volumes in 1930–1931. Meanwhile her comparative study of Thomism was slowly assuming comprehensive proportions. Just at this time, an offer arrived from the Educational Institute in Mün-ster. Out of respect for the ongoing negotiations with the universities, Edith Stein did not immediately reply. That the desire for prestige was not the motive behind the delay clearly emerges from a letter she sent to a friend:

> Until the study is finished, I'd like to put off coming to
> Freiburg. I don't know what will happen after that. Perhaps if

[6] Report of Professor Schulemann, Edith-Stein-Archiv, Karmel Köln.

the offer from the Educational Institute had come sooner, I would simply drop the whole idea of the *Habilitation* altogether. From the start, the study has meant more to me for itself than for any practical purpose it might serve. Anyway, God knows what he has in mind for me; that's something I don't need to worry about.[7]

The attitude reflected in this letter is confirmed by the description of a woman who made her acquaintance at this time on retreats at Saint Lioba. "She was so completely unassuming that you barely noticed she was there. She never made herself the center of attention. And yet, from the first moment, you couldn't help feeling the spell of the great holiness that emanated from her tranquil personality."[8]

Edith Stein decided to accept the position at Münster. Before moving there in the spring of 1932, she again spoke to Abbot Walzer of her persistent desire to enter contemplative life. The abbot insisted that the Church in Germany needed the contribution she would make in Münster. Such was also the opinion expressed by Maria Wilkens, long-term president of the Association of German Catholic Women Teachers, in recalling her first encounter with Edith Stein:

I first remember meeting Edith Stein in Essen at the 1932 general assembly of the Association of German Catholic Women Teachers. I knew that she was a philosopher of note—an associate of Husserl, the founder of phenomenology—and that she had made a radical conversion to Catholicism, to the point of abandoning her secular career in philosophy. . . . I admired her for her contribution to philosophy, her superb presentations at the Salzburg Hochschule Conventions and the congresses of the Association of Catholic University Graduates and the Catholic Women's League, and her profound reflections on "Woman's Role in the Light of Nature and Grace" and

[7] Stein, *Briefe I,* Letter 89, pp. 86–87.
[8] Teresia Renata Posselt, *Edith Stein. Eine Grosse Frau unseres Jahrhunderts,* 9th ed. (Freiburg-Basel-Vienna: Herder, 1963), p. 83.

"Woman in Professional Life". It made me happy to see a woman of such intellectual prominence so deeply committed to the ideals of the Catholic women's movement. We were proud that Professor Steffens and Maria Schmitz had managed to obtain for the Institute the woman from whom Catholic Germany was expecting so much—especially as it was the Federation of Catholic Teachers and the Association of German Catholic Women Teachers that supported the Institute. We hoped that eventually it would lead to a university professorship for her.[9]

It was with some misgiving that Edith Stein took on her duties. Apart from the uncertainty she felt about the overall direction of her lectures, she was afraid that her long "leave of absence" from professional philosophy might create insuperable obstacles in relating to her students and colleagues. Her fears proved groundless, and soon she was writing delightedly to a friend:

> I'm so pleased to find that, gradually, relations with faculty and students are becoming closer. (The "gradually" is entirely on my part, because of the limited time I can afford for it.) Officers from two of the student groups, as well as from the Saint Elizabeth Association, have already visited me to invite me to their meetings. I recently led an evening's discussion on women's issues at one of them that provoked quite a lively response. This is the sort of thing that might be able to attract students from the university as auditors, which would be beneficial for both sides.[10]

At meetings like the one mentioned above, Edith Stein presented the Catholic position without compromise. Often, her manner alone would win her the admiration of her young listeners. "Her whole being radiated a kind of concentrated energy", one of them remembered. "Obviously, she possessed

---

[9] Maria Wilkens, "Erinnerungen an Edith Stein", in *Katholische Frauenbildung* 63. Jg. 1962, Heft 12, pp. 840–41.

[10] Stein, *Briefe I,* Letter 116, p. 111.

that rare quality of inner reserve which belongs only to individuals with a rich interior life."[11] The students in Münster quickly found out what had long been familiar to students in Speyer: that for Edith Stein, human beings took precedence over abstract knowledge.

> All her spare time was lovingly placed at her students' disposal. They enjoyed attending her lectures and eagerly assimilated the encouraging suggestions she offered about leading a truly authentic Catholic life. She regarded this work with college-age youth as her God-given task, to which she had sacrificed her yearning to consecrate herself to God in the religious life. . . . All of us considered her a model, both of humanity at its purest and noblest and of a life lived out of Christian conviction. She always concealed that great erudition of hers beneath the veil of an equally great modesty.[12]

Living at the Collegium Marianum, a house of studies for young religious in Münster, Edith Stein was frequently called on to extend her apostolate into her time of prayer. Sometimes, in the midst of her busy schedule, she would yearn to go apart for a while and celebrate her "silent liturgy" (her name for private prayer) or share in the fullness of the divine praises at Beuron. Instead, her special sensitivity and skill led to even further demands on her time and energy. Some of her Jewish friends began to seek her out as a person who could help them on their journey to Christ. One of them, a childhood companion, recalled the transformation that she observed: "What a change there had been in Edith! Now, instead of the old ambitious drive, there was a tranquil maturity about her; the egotism had given way to a new sympathy and kindness. She seemed to have an unlimited supply of patience for discussing things, whether personal problems, questions of belief, or issues of philosophy. We felt very close to each other."[13] Edith

[11] Posselt, *Edith Stein*, p. 87.
[12] Ibid., p. 89.
[13] Ibid., p. 81.

Stein attempted to offer the same kind of generous, unaffected attention to all her friends. Rather than allowing her learning and piety to form a barrier, she used her intellectual and spiritual gifts to help maintain familiarity with their concerns. As a friend from Göttingen wrote:

> On the two occasions when I visited her in Münster, where I was most cordially welcomed by the sisters, she took the greatest interest in my work. She never played the part of the recluse who had withdrawn from the world: every detail of my family's life interested her deeply. Being with her was always a blessing for me; I always came away a little bit richer—either my own thoughts grew clearer, or I came to see an old problem in a new light. She was especially good with children. She knew just the right way to play with them while having a marvelous time herself. My son, born in 1923, was particularly dear to her. He came with me twice to Münster and then once later on to Cologne, where he kissed her through the grille, even though he couldn't stand it.[14]

Yet, whatever personal fulfillment she may have experienced dedicating herself to the inner well-being of her neighbor, academically Edith Stein found the work in Münster frustrating. She expressed this dissatisfaction in a letter she wrote to Freiburg in the summer of 1932: "I'm in the middle of a somewhat difficult battle to justify my scholarly existence. Not with anyone here—they're all doing everything they can to help me—but with the general situation which has resulted from my ten-year hiatus from work of this sort and my deeply-rooted lack of identity with contemporary life."[15] It had been one thing to teach in the tranquil environment of a convent school with the opportunity for part-time scholarly research on the side; it was another to bear the major responsibility for constructing a new educational theory on theological and philosophical lines. Rather than immediately

---

[14] Edith-Stein-Archiv, Karmel Köln.
[15] Stein, *Briefe I,* Letter 116, pp. 110–11.

proceeding to an in-depth examination of current issues, Edith Stein offered her colleagues a preliminary series of lectures on philosophical anthropology in an attempt to situate the mystery of the human person for them in the context of the European tradition. Such clarification of key concepts was absolutely necessary, given their diverse intellectual backgrounds. With her relentless self-criticism to protect her, she was not afraid of succumbing to presumption. The interior struggle this effort created reflected itself in letters to Hedwig Conrad-Martius, to whom she looked for sympathy and support:

> Have you ever tried to figure out exactly what pedagogy is? You can't come to a clear understanding of it until the fundamental presuppositions have been clarified. And we all come from such different philosophical backgrounds (or, in the case of the psychologist, from none at all) that you can imagine how difficult it is for us to come to any agreement. The one thing we are agreed on is the goal: the formulation of a Catholic educational theory. That in itself is quite worthwhile, and I'm grateful we have that much in common.
>
> I'm learning a great deal myself in the process. All that hinders me is my own abysmal ignorance (especially in pedagogical theory and the history of philosophy) and the feeling that I'll never be able to make up for it. But I take consolation from the thought that, here in this commission, I can furnish some stimuli which others can make fruitful later on, despite the inadequacy of my own efforts.[16]

In another letter, she described an educational conference she attended in Berlin where she had vigorously challenged some of the fundamental notions of her fellow participants. She wanted to be sure there was at least substantial agreement regarding major issues before she would consider publishing her own insights. The conference left her with a sense of isolation. Despite the admiration and esteem her contribution had

[16] Ibid., Letter 135, pp. 131–32.

aroused, she felt out of place among people whose life and
work were so organically joined. "I see now that I've completely lost touch with the outside world . . . , as far as the
world is concerned, I've become absolutely useless. . . . I'm
very grateful to have gotten your essay. It clarifies for me once
again what real philosophical thinking is—and what my own
limits are. Over the last few months, this knowledge of my
own limits has been rapidly progressing."[17]

Participation in the 1932 conference on phenomenology and
Thomism of the Societé Thomiste at Juvisy only strengthened
her in this conviction, for all the acclaim she received there.
She failed to notice that, surrounded by leading representatives
of neoscholasticism from France, Belgium, and Germany, it
was she who led the discussion on the relation between the two
schools of thought. To everyone else it was apparent, as demonstrated by the words of her friend, Professor Rosenmöller:
"Although it was natural that she should have the best understanding of Husserl's method, given the fact that she had
served for a number of years as his assistant in Freiburg, still,
the clarity with which she expressed her ideas, even in French
when it was necessary, created an unusually strong impression
within this scholarly elite."[18]

The situation in Münster was no different. Though her
friends might praise her poise, her method, and her learning,
she herself was attempting to discover a way to withdraw
from academics altogether.

> Coming to terms with this is not something that depresses
> me—better this than holding a responsible position for which
> I lack so many of the prerequisites as well as the chance of ever
> making them up. For quite some time I've been resigned to the
> fact that anything I do from now on is destined to be even more
> fragmentary than all human endeavors are bound to be by their
> very nature. My one hope is that I can provide a push in the

[17] Ibid., Letter 126, p. 123.
[18] Posselt, *Edith Stein*, pp. 91–92.

direction that needs to be followed and that others will make a better job of it.[19]

The direction she referred to was no less than the establishment of new foundations for philosophical thinking that did not rest on the traditional forms of discourse. In trying to work out this "positive" orientation to metaphysics, she drew inspiration from the accomplishment of Thomas Aquinas. Like him, she wanted "to establish a philosophical and theological basis for comprehending all reality in the context of revealed truth".[20] Her plan was to give a "forward push" to contemporary philosophy that would simultaneously enable it to retain its links to the *philosophia perennis*.[21]

Perhaps her frame of mind at this time is summarized best by the letter she wrote to the Benedictine Petrus Winrath, responding to his critique of her Saint Thomas translation:

> No one could be more convinced than I am that there were other people better suited for the task. Had I understood from the start the difficulties that were involved, there's a good chance that I never even would have attempted it. I began it as a novice in scholasticism (though not in philosophy) with the primary intention of familiarizing myself with Thomas' thought. To me it seems almost a miracle that, given the circumstances, the work is actually finished and has turned out as well as it has—for all its shortcomings. I was able to work on it only in bits of time saved up from a full teaching schedule and other obligations, without any advisors or scholarly resources to rely on. As for the more extensive commentary you mentioned, it was something for which I lacked the necessary competence. Maybe the purpose of having an unsuspecting little David like myself attack Goliath first was to give an incentive to the warriors in full armor.

---

[19] Stein, *Briefe I,* Letter 126, p. 123 and Letter 139, p. 135.

[20] Ibid., Letter 126, p. 123.

[21] *Philosophia perennis* is the investigation of the primary questions of ontology and epistemology that has consistently characterized classical Western thought. —TRANS.

What I would like to do, if I were fifteen or twenty years younger, would be to begin the study of philosophy all over again. At my age, however, I have the obligation to make my work bear fruit—and I have to leave everything else to my spare moments. I hope you will allow me to write you occasionally for your suggestions. Over and above that, I ask you to remember my work in your prayers.[22]

---

[22] Ibid., Letter 117, p. 112.

Chapter 11

Anti-Semitic Persecution

During the previous decade, Edith Stein had conscientiously kept up contact with Husserl, who continued to take an active interest in his former student's development. It pained him that she could not give an unqualified assent to his thinking, but he did his best to respect and appreciate her point of view. Because of the open communication between them, Edith Stein was able to express candidly her reservations when she visited the elderly philosopher and his wife in Freiburg in 1930. This very candor, however, only proved to highlight their differences—especially in the area of religion. As often before, Edith Stein was confronted with the futility of discussion in achieving interior change. She recognized that prayer and personal sacrifice functioned as much more effective instruments. So she wrote to another of Husserl's former students, Sister Adelgundis Jaegerschmid:

> I suppose it is good to be able to speak freely with him about ultimate questions. And yet, not only does it increase his own level of responsibility, it also heightens our responsibility for him. Prayer and sacrifice, in my opinion, are much more crucial than anything we can say. . . . It's very possible that he could be a "chosen instrument" without being in a state of grace. I don't mean that we should judge him, and of course we have every right to hope in God's unfathomable mercy. On the other hand, we have no right to conceal how serious the issues are. After every meeting with him, I come away convinced of

my inability to influence him directly and feeling the urgent necessity of offering some holocaust of my own for him.[1]

Political circumstances kept the idea of a sacrifice in the forefront of her thinking. In Münster, two years later, Edith Stein looked on horrified as university students began violently attacking Jews. A patriotic German herself, she had always been proud of her Jewish heritage. Baptism had further sharpened her understanding of her people's special vocation. Now she felt dazed. Unconcerned for her own safety, she suffered intensely over those being victimized by racial hatred and worried about her family and friends in Breslau. Her grief manifested itself visibly.

> Though she never complained outwardly [one student wrote], nevertheless it was heartrending to have to see her gentle face contorted in pain. Her features had started to take on the traces of the mystery later expressed by her religious name: Teresa Benedicta of the Cross. I can still hear her saying, "One day this will all have to be atoned for." I have no doubt that even then she saw the punishment that would be visited on our poor nation.[2]

Seeking to come to terms with her people's tragic destiny—Edith Stein was one of the few who recognized the final outcome right from the beginning—she turned to the Cross. Her friend Sister Adelgundis recalled an incident of that year in Freiburg, when, "after looking at the crucifix on the wall and asking me to look at it with her, she made a comparison—I no longer remember the exact words—between the divine sacrifice of the Cross and the terrible path of suffering awaiting the Jewish people."[3] Anti-Semitic persecution was pushing Edith

[1] Edith Stein, *Selbstbildnis in Briefen* I. Teil 1916–1934, Edith Steins Werke, Bd. VIII (Druten: De Maas und Waler/Freiburg-Basel-Vienna: Herder, 1976), Letter 52, p. 60.

[2] Teresia Renata Posselt, *Edith Stein. Eine Grosse Frau unseres Jahrhunderts,* 9th ed. (Freiburg-Basel-Vienna: Herder, 1963), p. 90.

[3] Edith-Stein-Archiv, Karmel Köln.

Stein closer to the realization of her unique vocation, the merging of Judaism and Christianity into a single redemptive unity. The words she spoke to her Jesuit confessor, Father Hirschmann, shortly before her martyr's death, demonstrate her appreciation of this special mission: "You don't know what it means to me to be a daughter of the chosen people—to belong to Christ, not only spiritually, but according to the flesh."[4]

In 1932, Edith Stein met Mother Petra Brüning, superior of the Ursuline nuns in Dorsten. She spoke to the sister about her desire for religious life and her other concerns, and, in response, Mother Petra invited her to visit Dorsten for Christmas. At Dorsten, Edith Stein spent the whole of Christmas Eve praying in church. Later she explained to the anxious superior, "How could anyone feel sleepy on a night like this?"[5] Immediately at home in the atmosphere of the religious house, Edith Stein wrote the following January to express her gratitude for Mother Petra's generous hospitality:

> I would like to express my heartfelt thanks again for those quiet, relaxing days at Christmas, especially for all the time you set aside for me. I admit that there was more to my coming to Dorsten than the simple desire to pass the holy days in the solitude of the cloister: I sensed that there was an inner bond between us and that it would be important to meet you face-to-face. . . . The trip to Berlin is now over and done with. From the external point of view, it seems to have been a success, and I'm grateful to all those who supported me with their prayers. What kind of a lasting effect it will have is impossible to predict. The experience on the whole was an exhausting one and proved to me once more what a serious responsibility we have before us. . . . Since Monday night, I've been back to my normal schedule at the Marianum, as much as a normal schedule can be spoken of, given my situation. Thank goodness, the greatest part of the winter is now over.[6]

[4] Ibid.
[5] Stein, *Briefe I,* Letter 130, p. 126, and Letter 133, p. 129.
[6] Ibid., Letter 130, p. 126.

It looks like I'll be staying in Münster through all of March. I
wanted to tell you how much it means to me that you consider
me as a member of the *corpus monasticum* and that, to your
thinking, the habit isn't the essential thing. That in itself makes
me feel as if I were somehow already part of convent life. God
has been making his intentions for me particularly apparent
again over the last few weeks; I see what I have to do with much
more clarity and distinctness. Granted this includes an ever-
deepening insight into my own inadequacy, it also means seeing the possibility of being God's instrument in spite of it.[7]

The drastic political changes of 1933 finally resolved the issue of Edith Stein's vocation. Along with the Nazi takeover
there came a large-scale offensive against the Jews. Thousands
were forced to leave their jobs and businesses without warning; unsuspecting citizens were violently attacked. Hitler used
his rearmament program, his reduction of unemployment,
and his appeal to national pride to blind large segments of the
population. They looked to the Führer to lead them to a better
future, though those with more foresight saw in his carefully
fomented anti-Semitism the prelude to an all-out battle against
Christianity and every other form of spiritual autonomy. Initially, Edith Stein's position as a Catholic at a Catholic Institute seemed relatively secure, but a visit to the home of a
colleague soon taught her otherwise. While they were at dinner, the head of the household, not knowing that she was Jewish, began to describe in great detail the anti-Jewish outbursts
that were taking place.

I had heard even before this of different measures being taken
against Jews. But now, all of a sudden, I realized that God had
once more laid a heavy hand upon his people—my people. The
man sitting across from me didn't have the least idea of what
was going on inside me. . . . To have told him and possibly
robbed him of his night's sleep would only have been a viola-
tion of his hospitality.[8]

[7] Ibid., Letter 133, p. 129.
[8] Posselt, *Edith Stein,* p. 97.

Edith Stein felt called to take action on behalf of her people. She submitted a request for a private papal audience, hoping that a special encyclical would alleviate the situation. Yet interiorly, she remained dissatisfied. "Though it was completely in character for me to get involved in such an undertaking, I couldn't help feeling that I hadn't yet made my individual contribution. What that contribution consisted of, however, I still had no idea."[9]

At Easter, while traveling to Beuron to consult with Abbot Walzer, Edith Stein interrupted her journey to attend a Holy Hour at the Carmelite convent in Cologne. During the service, she found her attention wandering from the homilist's words.

> I spoke with the Savior to tell him that I realized it was his Cross that was now being laid upon the Jewish people, that the few who understood this had the responsibility of carrying it in the name of all, and that I myself was willing to do this, if he would only show me how. I left the service with the inner conviction that I had been heard, but uncertain as ever as to what "carrying the Cross" would mean for me.[10]

When she returned to Münster, Edith Stein learned that her request for an audience had been refused. She sent her appeal in writing to the Pope, who responded with a benediction for herself and her family. Edith Stein realized that most people could not grasp the urgency of the threat as she did. Even Abbot Walzer distrusted her grim premonitions. Yet her alarm proved wholly justified: scarcely had she come back to Münster, when she was told that she would have to give up her position. A sympathetic administration suggested working on her projects privately until the general situation improved, but she declined.

An offer to teach in South America also awaited her in Münster. After giving the matter serious consideration, Edith Stein became convinced that the time had at last come for fulfilling

[9] Ibid., p. 98.
[10] Ibid., p. 100.

her hopes to enter the convent. She described her decision in her diary:

> Toward the end, waiting had become very hard for me; I felt like a stranger in the world. Even before beginning my work in Münster, I had pleaded [with Abbot Walzer] for permission to enter the convent, which he had refused me on the grounds of my mother's reaction and my own contribution to Catholic life. And I had submitted. But now, the walls of resistance were caving in. My effectiveness had come to an end, and as far as my mother was concerned, wouldn't she prefer seeing me in a German convent than in a South American school so far away?
>
> On April 30 (Good Shepherd Sunday that year), I attended part of the Thirteen Hours devotion which Saint Ludger's parish was celebrating in honor of its patronal feast. I arrived in the afternoon, determined not to leave until I found out if I could now enter Carmel. Just as the concluding blessing was being given, I felt the Good Shepherd giving me his consent.[11]

It was the first moment in yet another stage of Edith Stein's spiritual journey, one that would be characterized by "the peace of someone who has reached her goal".[12]

At Pentecost, several weeks after this incident, she wrote to Hedwig Conrad-Martius, "There's nothing to regret about the fact that I can't continue to lecture. To me a great and merciful Providence seems to be standing behind it all. Actually, I think I see the resolution fairly clearly myself, but I'm still not free to communicate it to you."[13] Edith Stein was speaking of her application to the Carmelite convent in Cologne. Though she worried that she might be considered too old (she was forty-two), the sisters were impressed with her, and in mid-June they notified her of her acceptance.

Hard as it was for her to leave Münster and her friends, it was the confrontation with her family that Edith Stein dreaded. She confessed this anxiety in a letter to a friend:

[11] Ibid.
[12] Ibid., p. 101.
[13] Stein, *Briefe I*, Letter 143, p. 139.

I'll be staying with my mother from the middle of August to the middle of September, so I can have time to prepare her gradually. She already knows that I plan to live with the nuns in Cologne, but I've never written to tell her that I intend to enter the convent. As things stand, I'm supposed to be received as a postulant on October fifteenth. I'll let you know how it all came to pass when you come to visit me at the grille—It's quite amazing. . . .

As you can imagine, the manuscript doesn't concern me all that much anymore. Please keep it for yourself—I have two other copies anyway and would be happy to think that you were getting some use out of it.

I ask you to join me in thanking God for the great grace of this extraordinary vocation, and I also ask for your prayers during the coming months in Breslau. . . . If things in general weren't so awful, I personally would be grateful to them [the National Socialists] for having finally opened the way for me. Thank goodness, my relatives are taking the situation calmly. Once I'm inside the calm of a cloistered community, I hope I can be a greater help to them.[14]

Christians themselves often have trouble understanding the value of a contemplative vocation; for the Steins it was an impossibility. The day came when Frau Stein asked her daughter, "What do you plan on doing with the sisters in Cologne?" When Edith answered "Join them",[15] peace at home was a thing of the past. Everyone in the family felt crushed by the tragedy. Edith herself clung to her friends to keep from faltering in her decision; her mother, not daring to display her anger openly, wept in desperation; the brothers and sisters did all they could to change their sister's mind. "Why did you have to get to know him?" demanded Frau Stein. "He was a good man—I'm not saying anything against him. But why did he have to go and make himself God?"[16]

In this struggle between mother and daughter, Church and Synagogue met in symbolic confrontation. To the eighty-

[14] Ibid., Letter 146, p. 143.
[15] Posselt, *Edith Stein,* p. 106.
[16] Ibid., p. 108.

four-year-old Frau Stein, it seemed as if her daughter wished to desert her just at the moment when Jews in Germany were undergoing bitter persecution. Edith Stein recognized the impossible nature of the situation. She knew there was no explanation that would satisfy her mother. Her friends and colleagues came forward with sympathy and advice, but they could not help her. "It was a step that had to be taken in the absolute darkness of faith. Time and again, I asked myself during those weeks, 'Which of us is going to break first—me or my mother?' But the two of us held out to the very last day."[17]

That last day at home was her birthday, October 12. Once again, it was a Jewish holiday, this time the final day of the Feast of Booths. Edith Stein spent it in synagogue with her mother. In the evening, some friends dropped by to say farewell. Once they had left,

> my mother buried her face in her hands and began to cry. I stood behind her chair, resting her old, white-haired head against my chest. We stayed like that for a long time, until I was able to convince her to go up to bed. After taking her upstairs and helping her to undress—for the first time in her life—I sat alongside her at the edge of the bed until she sent me off to sleep. But I don't think either one of us got any sleep that night.[18]

The next morning, still utterly unable to comprehend her decision, the family bowed to the inevitable. As she boarded the train in a state of total emotional exhaustion, Edith Stein felt like someone awaking from a horrible dream. Slowly, her thoughts turned to Cologne: "Now it was really happening after all—what I had scarcely dared hope for. I couldn't feel any violent upsurge of enthusiasm over it: I had just been through something too terrible for that. But I did feel a great sense of calm, knowing that I was coming into the harbor of God's will."[19]

[17] Ibid., p. 107.
[18] Ibid., p. 108.
[19] Ibid., p. 109.

Chapter 12

In the Cologne Carmel

"She ran to Carmel, singing for joy, like a child to its mother's arms, never doubting her almost blind enthusiasm for even an instant. It reminded me of the way Saint Benedict speaks of our journey to God: 'Now we must run and do the things that will profit us forever.' "[1] In these words Abbot Walzer expressed his surprise at the speed with which Edith Stein settled into her new environment. His fear had been that, once in Carmel, she would grow restive within the confines of the enclosure, surrounded by sisters of limited academic background. Fortunately events did not bear him out. Edith Stein neither worried about the austerities and restrictions of Carmelite life nor looked for permission to do scholarly work. Her vocation to Carmel was genuine; no hidden motive obscured the purity of her intention. When she arrived at the convent, it was with full understanding that the whole of the Carmelite vocation consisted in the individual's response to God's claim of love. She had learned this studying the life of Thérèse of Lisieux, of whom she spoke in a letter of 1933: "My impression was, that this was a life which had been absolutely transformed by the love of God, down to the last detail. I simply can't imagine anything greater. I would like to see this attitude incorporated

---

[1] Teresia Renata Posselt, *Edith Stein. Eine Grosse Frau unseres Jahrhunderts,* 9th ed. (Freiburg-Basel-Vienna: Herder, 1963), p. 125.

as much as possible into my own life and the lives of those who are dear to me."[2]

With respect to her new sisters, right from the beginning she felt entirely at home with them: "Best of all," she wrote, "the spirit of Carmel is love, and that spirit is very much alive in our community."[3]

For all her unbounded generosity, there were certain things that constituted quite a struggle for the forty-two-year-old postulant. This is reflected in her later article about Katharina Esser, a distinguished nineteenth-century Cologne Carmelite:

> It was no small sacrifice for the forty-six-year-old woman, long accustomed to managing her own existence, to become a child for a second time and submit her judgment to that of her superiors. Years later, she openly avowed that she had found it a bitter experience. "It is easier to be nailed to the Cross with the Savior than to become an obedient child with him", was the way she had put it. And yet she succeeded.[4]

Essentially, what Edith Stein, philosopher and educational specialist, had to learn in Carmel was how to become a pupil. While it is true that she had always been unusually receptive to the masters of the intellectual and spiritual life, first taking Husserl as her teacher and later receiving "guidance" from Teresa of Avila and Thomas Aquinas, nevertheless, in her private life, she had always kept control, and her intellectual authority had gone largely unchallenged. Now it was different. She found herself in a situation where people twenty years her junior were carrying out their duties more effectively than she. Her advice was no longer asked for; to the rest of the commu-

---

[2] Edith Stein, *Selbstbildnis in Briefen* I. Teil 1916–1934, Edith Steins Werke, Bd. VIII (Druten: De Maas and Waler/Freiburg-Basel-Vienna: Herder, 1976), Letter 137, p. 133.

[3] Ibid., Letter 147, p. 144.

[4] Edith Stein, "Eine deutsche Frau und grosse Karmelitin: Mutter Franziska von den unendlichen Verdiensten Jesu Christi, O.C.D. (Katharina Esser) 1804–1866", in *Die in Deinem Hause wohnen*, ed. P. Eugen Lense (Einsiedeln and Cologne: Verlag Benziger, 1938), p. 157.

nity, she simply appeared as a rather clumsy postulant. Most of the sisters had no idea of the previous history or accomplishments of their newest member.[5] They were absorbed in living the austere existence of apostolic love and humble service that their foundress, Teresa of Avila, had fashioned for them—and Teresa had insisted that nothing be allowed to distract the sisters from fixing their minds on God.

Yet despite the demands of the transition, Edith Stein blossomed in the happy novitiate atmosphere. Her face lost the traces of former suffering and acquired a cheerful new serenity. She succeeded in adapting herself to her younger companions and patiently accepted her own limitations. Initially, it was the complicated ceremonies and usages of community life that she found particularly troublesome. Somehow her mind would not retain them. Then there was the manual labor, for which her long years of intellectual activity had not prepared her. As she wrote in mock despair to Mother Petra:

> For the time being, I try to keep telling myself how displeased you would be with the way I pray the Office. I seem to be a fairly awkward novice altogether, who puts a strain on the love and patience of the superiors and the rest of the community. Clearly, it will be some time until they can make a passable nun out of me. So please pray that I can learn to correspond to the great grace of this vocation.[6]

A more positive evaluation of Edith Stein's early months in Carmel was offered by one of her fellow novices:

> Though I couldn't have told you at first glance exactly how old Edith Stein was, her hair which was going gray at the temples gave me a pretty good idea. It didn't surprise me at all when I found out a few days later that she was forty-two. But she behaved just like the rest of us, without looking for any privileges: her simple, natural modesty was something beyond exaggeration. She quickly lost her solemn look—which made

---

[5] Posselt, *Edith Stein*, pp. 112–13.
[6] Stein, *Briefe I*, Letter 159, p. 155.

her seem about twenty years younger—and she also began being more approachable instead of so distant and reserved. So it didn't take long until all of us felt as if we had always been together. Over the next few weeks, we learned a little more about Edith Stein's Jewish background and her past achievements. That did surprise me, and my surprise grew greater the better I got to know this woman so totally devoted to God.

One of the things that struck me most about her was her devotion to prayer. The liturgy held her spellbound; at Mass, she seemed to participate as if she were offering herself on the altar. She was very zealous about the Divine Office. On Sundays and holidays, when our schedule permitted it, she would spend hours at a time praying in front of the Blessed Sacrament. My impression was that once she had entered into these intimate conversations with God, time and space ceased to exist.

Another thing I noticed was her respect for the younger sisters. You could see the love and humility with which she tried to adapt to us. It was only years later that I discovered how difficult the adaptation had been. When she told me about her problems adjusting, I couldn't imagine what she meant, so I began telling her about my own troubles in settling down to Carmel as a twenty-year-old. "I don't doubt it", she answered. "But novitiate can be terribly trying on someone of forty, too. The only difference is that it would be another set of problems." If she hadn't said it herself, I wouldn't have ever believed it. It all seemed to come so naturally to her. When I remember the reverence she paid to superiors!

She was just as faithful about obeying the novitiate regulations as she was observing the other practices of the Rule. Our novice mistress had been a little worried at first when she heard she would have to teach a scholar. But Edith Stein was so amiable and eager to learn that the novice mistress soon forgot her nervousness. Edith Stein always thought of herself as someone who had a lot to learn. There was one time I can remember, when she had to miss a novitiate class, due to the visit of a philosopher friend who came to consult her on some matter. When she joined us at recreation that evening, the first thing she asked was, "Did you learn anything interesting in novitiate today?" Without waiting an instant, I said to her, "That's how it is. When you're not there, you don't hear." But she, with her quick wit, replied, "Yes, but it says in the Bible, 'Wisdom I learned without guile, and I imparted it without grudging' " (Wis 7:13). That hit home, and after I told her about the material we covered, I thought to myself, "I don't know if she realizes it, but Edith Stein has just described herself in the words of the Scripture." That's how simple and straightforward she was in everything.

When it came to housework, she was always making all kinds of mistakes on account of her lack of practical experience. Though novitiate custom demanded that each one of these had to be paid for with a reprimand or admonition, there wasn't a single time that I saw her display the least bit of irritation over it. She took correction with a humility that was genuinely edifying. It was clear that she wanted to use these occasions as a means of growing in holiness. No matter how often they happened she never lost her good-humored smile. But that shouldn't lead to the conclusion that she was an impassive sort of person whom nothing could affect. She had quite a lively temperament, and her passionate side sometimes showed itself in her beautiful, flashing eyes. It was simply that she kept her whole personality under the control of a strict self-discipline that was never relaxed for an instant.

Everyone knows that more laughing and joking goes on in novitiate than anywhere else. Novices laugh about anything — or, for that matter, about nothing at all. Edith Stein joined wholeheartedly in the fun. Sometimes she laughed so hard — especially when the joke was on her — that the tears rolled down her cheeks. Yet, at a certain point in the novitiate, when I was feeling depressed, it was Edith Stein who, as inconspicuously as possible, did everything she could to cheer me up. She found all kinds of opportunities for doing me favors or whispering a word of encouragement. She had a genius for coming up with exactly the right thing. All because, for love of Christ, she wanted to be "all things to all men".

Once in a while, at recreation, she would tell us something about the events of her past life. As she spoke, you could feel the closeness there was between herself, her Orthodox mother, and all her brothers and sisters. There was something about her

that inspired confidence and made you want to share her dedication. Even when it came to little things, she was always
practicing obedience and trying to put aside her own wishes.[7]

Edith Stein had entered the Carmelites in the hope of living
up to the ideal contained in her article on Teresa of Avila:
"Only the person who renounces self-importance, who no
longer struggles to defend or assert himself, can be large
enough for God's boundless action."[8] For years before her entry, she had tried to prepare for the sacrifices religious life
would entail:

> In the childhood of the spiritual life, when we first entrust our-
> selves to God's providence, God's guiding hand feels very
> strong and firm. We know as clear as day what we should or
> shouldn't do. But things don't stay like this forever. Anyone
> who belongs to Christ is destined to pass through all the stages
> of his life—up to and including his adulthood and, eventually,
> even to the way of the Cross that leads to Gethsemane and Gol-
> gotha. When that hour comes, external sufferings are nothing
> compared to the dark night of the soul, when the divine light
> stops shining and the divine voice stops speaking. It isn't that
> God isn't there, but that he's concealed and silent. Why, you
> ask. That is one of God's secrets, and no one can fully penetrate
> it. . . . Each of us is perpetually on the razor's edge: on one
> side, absolute nothingness; on the other, the fullness of divine
> life.[9]

Now that she had been accepted into the convent, Edith Stein
resolved to embrace her vocation as generously as possible.

With the initial adjustment behind her, Edith Stein began
looking forward to the day of her Clothing, when she would
be given the habit of the order. It was not a wholly unclouded
time: the continuing conflict with her mother tinged the prep-

---

[7] Report of Sr. Electa, Edith-Stein-Archiv, Karmel Köln.

[8] Edith Stein, "Eine Meisterin der Erziehungs- und Bildungsarbeit: Teresia
von Jesus", in *Katholische Frauenbildung im deutschen Volk,* 48 Jg., February
1935, pp. 122–23.

[9] Edith Stein, "Weihnachtsgeheimnis", in *Wege zur inneren Stille,* collected
articles, ed. W. Herbstrith (Frankfurt: Kaffke Verlag, 1978), p. 12.

arations with sorrow. She spoke of this in a letter to Mother Petra: "Please keep me in your prayers during the next few weeks. I have a feeling that there are some severe trials ahead of me before I can think of the habit as 'paid for'. Actually, they've started already: my mother is doing everything she can to block the ceremony. It's hard to watch her go through so much mental anguish, without being able, humanly speaking, to do anything to help her."[10]

Because Frau Stein regarded Edith's reception of the habit as the ultimate break between her daughter and the Jewish people, not only did she not attend the ceremony, for years afterward she refused to answer any of the weekly letters Edith mailed from Carmel. Nor were any of the brothers and sisters present, though some of them sent congratulations. But those who did attend the ceremony on April 15, 1934—the many friends and colleagues she had made over the years—had the privilege of seeing the new nun at her most radiantly happy. Gerda Krabbel, president of the Woman's Federation, exclaimed when she met her in her bridal dress, "I'm so glad to be here to see you like this. It is absolutely right."[11] The author Gertrud von le Fort was so impressed by Edith Stein's appearance that she kept a photo of her on her desk as an inspiration for her book, *The Eternal Woman*. Both these friends sensed something of the mystery Edith Stein was entering into, which she had described in one of her lectures: "The bride of Christ assumes a life of spiritual motherhood for all redeemed humanity. This is just as true whether she works directly with souls or whether, by sacrifice alone, she brings forth fruit hidden from both herself and from everyone else."[12]

For the religious name, traditionally taken on this day, Edith Stein chose Teresia Benedicta a Cruce—Teresa, Blessed

[10] Stein, *Briefe I,* Letter 165, p. 161.

[11] Edith Stein, *Selbstbildnis in Briefen* II. Teil 1934–1942, Edith Steins Werke, Bd. IX (Druten: De Maas und Waler/Freiburg-Basel-Vienna: Herder, 1977), Letter 171, p. 5.

[12] Edith Stein, *Frauenbildung und Frauenberufe,* collection of articles written after 1930, 4th ed. (Munich: Verlag Schnell und Steiner, 1956), p. 124.

of the Cross. She had sought out a name that would express her gratitude for the spiritual patronage of Saint Benedict and Saint Teresa and at the same time reflect her special devotion to the Passion of Christ. "Would you like to know my patron [she wrote to Mother Petra]? It's obviously holy Father Benedict. Even though I never even became a Benedictine Oblate — since all I could ever see ahead of me was Mount Carmel — he's been kind enough to adopt me and to make me an honorary member of his order."[13]

Abbot Walzer had come from Beuron to officiate at the ceremony and deliver the homily. It was one sermon that couldn't end soon enough for Edith Stein — so glowing a portrait of her did the abbot paint. Afterward, in the parlor, the abbot took her aside to find out how she was doing. He received a typically straightforward response: "She confirmed all my expectations. With characteristic ardor she let me know that at Carmel she felt absolutely at home — heart and soul. I wasn't tempted for a moment to see this as a miracle of grace. To me it was the completion of a process that was perfectly in line with her whole spiritual development."[14]

Soon after the celebration, she wrote to Mother Petra to thank her for her gift and reflect on the magnitude of what she had been given:

> If you only knew how little it takes to make us Carmelites happy! Your present overwhelmed us. So much love and kindness would embarrass me if I didn't know that they're meant more for my holy vocation — which I received through no merit of my own — than for me as an individual. As it is, I use each mark of affection as a stimulus for mustering up my spiritual resources in the hope of becoming a less unworthy *vas electionis*. . . .[15] Still, this poor little soul is so tiny compared to the abundance of grace that comes to it each day.[16]

---

[13] Stein, *Briefe II,* Letter 178, p. 13.

[14] Posselt, *Edith Stein,* p. 126.

[15] This Latin phrase means "chosen vessel". Cf. Acts 9:15.

[16] Stein, *Briefe I,* Letter 165, p. 160.

A second letter echoed the first: "To me, there's something almost more overpowering in being granted a request after long and persevering prayer than in receiving a response immediately. I'm still stunned by how gloriously my hopes have been fulfilled."[17]

Edith Stein did not consider her official incorporation into convent life as an excuse to become oblivious or unsympathetic to the needs of her neighbor. She worked at maintaining her correspondence with the friends and associates who depended on her advice. Writing to Mother Petra, she urged her to be completely frank in expressing her concerns.

> As a matter of fact, the more detailed the information you send us, the more inspired we feel to pray for the needs of our sisters in the world. It's also occurred to me that it might be good for you to come and spend a couple of days with us. We can't offer you anything very splendid: there's no imposing liturgy here or anything like that. All we have is our joyful poverty and our peace, which our kind of life makes so much easier to hold on to than it is for the people who have to face a daily, or even hourly, battle. I always feel so glad when someone can come here and build up a little strength for the conflict.[18]

As the political situation worsened, Edith Stein's Jewish friends began visiting the convent to discuss their plans for emigration. Invariably, they left the parlor strengthened and consoled. For Edith Stein, there was no contradiction between the demands of a life of prayer and the call to fraternal charity. Letters of hers repeatedly link the two:

> The one thing a person needs to keep doing is to try to live out his chosen vocation with an ever-increasing honesty and purity, to make it an acceptable oblation for those with whom he is united. We ourselves experience a constant stimulus to this in the tremendous confidence people place in us and the frighteningly high opinion many of them have of our vocation. . . .

[17] Stein, *Briefe II,* Letter 171, p. 5.
[18] Stein, *Briefe I,* Letter 165, p. 161.

The peace I experience every day seems too much of a gift to be meant for one person alone. I find great happiness, therefore, whenever someone arrives here all worn out and battered and then goes away with a measure of peace and consolation.[19]

While generously sharing the blessings of her contemplative vocation, Edith Stein was fully aware of the insecurity of her own position. Her political insight led her to expect the worst: as she told one visitor, it was more than likely that the Nazis would come and take her from the enclosure.

During the novitiate year, Edith Stein gradually returned to writing, in accord with her provincial's wishes. She completed the index for her translation of Saint Thomas and contributed to a number of periodicals. At the end of the year, the time came to pronounce her first religious vows. She wrote in anticipation to Hedwig Conrad-Martius: "I've just been approved for profession in April. Thank goodness, you don't have to be a 'finished product' for this, because, as far as I'm concerned, novitiate only really began a little while ago, once the adjustment to the externals—ritual, house custom, etc.— stopped taking up so much energy."[20]

Letters to Mother Petra convey a sense of her inner attitude as the time for her commitment approached:

If you insist on picturing me standing in choir, then please not in my white mantle. That's only worn at Communion and first-class solemnities. Think of me in the old brown habit, little and close to the ground as ever. It's the same story with my meditations. They're not any great, soaring spiritual flights, but very simple and down-to-earth. Their main value is that they express my gratitude at having this place as my earthly home.[21]

I get so much joy from the silent times here. Much as I love the Office and hate missing any of the choral hours, even the

[19] Ibid., Letter 164, pp. 159–60.
[20] Stein, *Briefe II,* Letter 189, p. 26.
[21] Ibid., Letter 182, p. 18.

little ones, our life rests on the two hours of silent meditation prescribed by the daily schedule. It's only now that I possess this blessing that I realize what I was missing before.[22]

Edith Stein pronounced her simple vows on Easter Sunday, 1935. Perhaps this is what inspired the answer she gave to the sister who asked her how she felt—"like the Bride of the Lamb."[23] Not long afterward, the nun had the pleasure of receiving a visit from Hedwig Conrad-Martius. Her old friend was forcibly struck by the change she observed in her fellow phenomenologist:

> That hour is indelibly engraved upon my memory. Though Edith had always been friendly and childlike, the aura of childlike happiness and contentment she now possessed was, if I may say so, absolutely charming. Grace and graciousness—the marvelous twofold sense of the word *gratia*—had come together to form a unity. . . . She told me with utter frankness about her difficulties in the novitiate year. And she had every right to do so, considering how much she had gained from them.[24]

In the Carmelite Order, three years normally separate the end of novitiate from the taking of solemn vows. Edith Stein's first major responsibility as a simply professed nun came in the form of a commission from her superiors to finish the manuscript of *Act and Potency* begun in Speyer. She wondered how she could accomplish the task. Her work would be frequently interrupted for the periods of common prayer. The manuscript stood in need of full-scale revision. The necessary scholarly resources and opportunities for consultation would not be available. Nonetheless, Edith Stein determined to do her best.

---

[22] Stein, *Briefe I,* Letter 168, p. 164.

[23] *Kölner Selig- und Heiligsprechungsprozess der Dienerin Gottes Sr. Teresia Benedicta a Cruce—Edith Stein,* eds. Teresia Renata Posselt, O.C.D., and Teresia Margareta Drügemöller, O.C.D. (Cologne, 1962), p. 17.

[24] Hedwig Conrad-Martius in *Edith Stein, Briefe an Hedwig Conrad-Martius* (Munich: Kösel-Verlag, 1960), p. 74.

It ended up taking all her hard-won self-discipline to learn how to break her concentration every time the bell was rung. She publicly admitted that she found it her severest penance. When Sunday came, her serious face would beam and she would say, "Thank God, I don't have to write today. Today I can pray."[25] Prior to entering the order, Edith Stein had attempted to work out the proper place of scholarship in the life of a Christian. She had written in her article "The Intellect and the Intellectual",

> The intellectual knows that supreme and ultimate truths do not manifest themselves through the workings of the human reason, and that when it comes to the most essential matters—those affecting the ordering of one's practical existence—it is possible for a higher degree of divine illumination to make a plain, uneducated person wiser than the most learned scholar.
>
> At the same time, the intellectual recognizes that the natural functioning of the human reason does have a legitimate domain, and this is where he applies his efforts. He is like a farmer tilling his fields: he knows what he does is both good and useful and yet fixed within certain limits, as is all human endeavor. Reason for him is like a carpenter's plane—whenever he can use it to help somebody, he is more than glad to be of service.[26]

Right from the start, Edith Stein had to battle with her old feelings of inadequacy. At difficult moments, she would write to Mother Petra:

> I'd also like to ask for your prayers. As of about a month ago, I've been assigned to some philosophical work. It's a major project, and I don't have access to a lot of the material that it requires. If I didn't believe in the blessing of obedience or trust that the Lord can use the weakest and most helpless instruments when he wants to, I think I'd drop out of the running

[25] Private communiqué.

[26] Edith Stein, "Der Intellekt und die Intellektuellen", in *Wege zur inneren Stille,* collected articles, ed. W. Herbstrith (Frankfurt: Kaffke Verlag, 1978), pp. 74–75.

completely. As it is, I do the best I can. There are times when my courage fails me at the thought of other people's erudition, but after I go to pray before the Blessed Sacrament it always revives.[27]

Sometimes she worked with so much intensity that her superiors began to worry about her health. Fortunately, visits from friends like Professor Alexander Koyré were able to provide a measure of relief. Their enthusiasm for her thesis helped counteract the anxiety she felt that she was placing too great a burden on her community by being dispensed from household duties. After one such visit from Hedwig Conrad-Martius, she wrote to thank her for her support: "It was something I needed badly. This kind of work doesn't easily fit into the framework of our life. It demands all kinds of sacrifices, not just from me, but from the rest of the sisters as well."[28]

Edith Stein completed her study in the summer of 1936. While waiting for an answer from the publishers to whom she had submitted the work (now entitled *Finite and Eternal Being*), she received the news of her mother's death. Frau Stein had died in Breslau on September 14, 1936, the Feast of the Holy Cross, after a long and painful struggle. Knowing the serious nature of her mother's illness, Edith Stein had written to many of her friends over the summer asking them to pray for the healing of her mother's embitterment. But Frau Stein had died despondent, unreconciled to her daughter's decision, despite the notes she had occasionally written in response to Edith's letters. The winter following Frau Stein's death, Edith had the joy of seeing her sister Rosa enter the Catholic Church. By coincidence, she was able to administer the final instructions as well as be present for the baptism: a broken wrist and ankle, the result of a fall down a flight of stairs, had forced her to be hospitalized outside the enclosure. On her return to the convent, she received her new assignment as house infirmarian.

---

[27] Stein, *Briefe II,* Letter 204, p. 42.
[28] Ibid., Letter 213, p. 50.

In 1937, the Cologne community celebrated an important anniversary. Three hundred years before, on November 5, 1637, the first group of Carmelites had arrived from Belgium to found a community in the city. They had remained until 1802, when, in the course of the Napoleonic conflict, they had been forced to leave the convent. Though the next generation had reestablished the community of Mary, Queen of Peace, they had not been able to regain possession of the former house. In commemoration of the tricentenary, Mother Teresia Renata Posselt, the prioress, along with Edith Stein and the house archivist, composed a chronicle of the community's varying fortunes. Little did they know that eight years later, at the end of the war, renovation would begin on the convent's original buildings.

One year after completion, *Finite and Eternal Being* still had no publisher, though the work had been submitted to a number of firms. Edith Stein was not unduly troubled. She wrote to Mother Petra:

> I don't know if I'll ever be able to compose anything on this scale again. For the moment, it looks as if I have entirely different responsibilities ahead of me. Whatever they are, I should be able to handle them as long as God provides the necessary ability. One thing is certain: it has to be good training in humility for me that I'm regularly assigned to tasks where all my efforts produce such unsatisfactory results. [29]

The new charge turned out to be answering the telephone. As busy as she found herself, regulating all the traffic between the convent and the outside world, she remained as tranquil and considerate as ever. One of the sisters observed:

> There's no way I could do justice to her kindness and generosity. She was never satisfied with carrying out the letter of the law; when love demanded it, she was always there, ready to lend a hand. *Ama, et fac quod vis.* [30] I think that must have been

[29] Ibid., Letter 254, p. 97.
[30] "Love and do what you will", is a saying of Saint Augustine. — TRANS.

her motto. I can't begin to tell you how many times she comforted and inspired me. On one evening when I was feeling very depressed, Edith Stein was in the pantry putting away the dishes. The great silence had already begun. I think she must have sensed my mood, because, even though she couldn't talk to me, she came over and gave me a beautiful, friendly smile. That's something I'll never forget. It made my troubles instantly vanish. She always stayed patient when things got hectic in the kitchen and she had to wait. She didn't want to cause any extra bother for anyone. . . . Once at recreation we started to talk about dying. I got all excited and called out, "When I die, the sisters have to sing a *Salve Regina!*" She looked thoughtfully at me and then, very seriously, she said "When I die, I think the sisters will be able to sing a *Te Deum.*"[31]

Death was a subject that began to assume increasing prominence in Edith Stein's thoughts. To a friend she wrote, "Though we would certainly have a lot to tell each other if you came for another visit, the important thing is to stay united in prayer so that we can meet again in the light of eternity. Every time I see someone go on ahead of me, my own yearning becomes all the greater."[32] Because of this sense of foreboding, Edith Stein was anxious to pronounce her solemn vows as soon as possible. "I've taken that beautiful picture of the Shroud of Turin you sent me as a gift from the Lord to help me get ready for solemn profession [she told Mother Petra]. I've put it right on the table of my cell where I'm able to look at it as often as I want."[33]

In 1937, Edith Stein received a visit from a foreign schoolteacher, Madame Renand. The report the woman left behind clarifies the reasons for her premonitions.

During that period, I happened to be spending a little time in the Rhineland. One of our school's philosophy instructors had asked me to gather information about Husserl, and when I

---

[31] Report of Sr. Electa, Edith-Stein-Archiv, Karmel Köln.
[32] Stein, *Briefe II,* Letter 224, p. 64.
[33] Ibid., Letter 254, p. 97.

went to consult Professor Dempf on the matter, he recommended visiting Edith Stein as the simplest way to go about it.

Edith Stein furnished me with a brilliant summary of Husserl's philosophy. Afterward, we spent some time talking together about Germany and the fateful times it was experiencing. She herself was expecting the worst and anticipated imminent disaster. Her earnest words testified to a lucid, powerful intellect, a profound faith, and an absolute reliance on God. Though I myself was simply a young, inexperienced schoolteacher at the time, she addressed me as candidly and affectionately as if I had been her younger sister. The whole meeting left me deeply impressed.[34]

Reports of deteriorating conditions abroad strengthened Edith Stein in her conviction: "The fate of our Spanish sisters teaches us what we ourselves have to be ready to expect", she wrote to a Dominican nun later that year. "When radical upheavals occur so close to home, they ought to be taken as a salutary warning."[35] With no illusions about the direction of political events, Edith Stein prepared to share the destiny of the Jewish people and travel along the way of the Cross. Like many of her friends who were attempting to emigrate, she developed tentative plans to move to Palestine in the belief that her transfer to the Carmel in Bethlehem would spare the convent danger.

In spite of the gathering darkness, 1938 fulfilled two of her dearest wishes: she was permitted to pronounce solemn vows, and she learned that Husserl, on his deathbed, had turned back to God. Husserl had fallen critically ill in the months before her profession. Shortly before the day of her vows (April 21, 1938—Thursday of Easter week), she wrote to Sister Adelgundis Jaegerschmid asking for news of the philosopher's condition:

Our letters cross from deathbed to deathbed. Today, after a year of suffering, our dear Sister Clara has gently passed into

---

[34] Report of Madame Renand, Edith-Stein-Archiv, Karmel Köln.
[35] Stein, *Briefe II,* Letter 238, p. 80.

eternal life. I've already recommended our dear Master to her protection and will do so again at the vigil tonight. He'll be in good company with her alongside him.

Sister Clara was our oldest laysister, tireless in carrying out the humblest tasks, yet with a masculine fortitude that enabled her to embrace and live out the Carmelite ideal with absolute determination. It was a life of faith, a completely spiritual life.

As regards my dear Master, I have no worries about him. To me, it has always seemed strange that God could restrict his mercy to the boundaries of the visible Church. God is truth, and whoever seeks the truth is seeking God, whether he knows it or not.[36]

What Edith Stein learned only after her vows was that, as of Holy Thursday, Husserl had turned from philosophy to God. Freed by his illness from scholarly obligations, he again experienced the attraction to Christ which for years had lain buried under philosophical problems. On Good Friday, his first words were, "Good Friday! What a wonderful day. Christ has forgiven us everything."[37] That evening, after a terrible struggle for breath, he said, "I have fervently prayed to God to let me die and he has given his consent. I find it a great disappointment that I am still alive. God is good—yes, good but so incomprehensible. It is a heavy trial for me. Light and darkness . . . deep darkness, and again light."[38] Husserl then tried to express his affection and gratitude to those who surrounded his bedside, after which he lapsed into a total silence. But shortly before his death on April 27, his face suddenly brightened, and he exclaimed, "Oh! I have seen something so wonderful. Quick, write it down!"[39] Before the nurse could return, however, Husserl had died and taken his mystery along with him.

[36] Ibid., Letter 259, p. 102.
[37] Adelgundis Jaegerschmid, O.S.B., "Die letzten Jahre Edmund Husserls", in *Stimmen der Zeit* 106 Jg., Band 199 (Freiburg, 1981), p. 137.
[38] Ibid., p. 138.
[39] Ibid.

Edith Stein received the report of the faith shown by the dying Husserl as a great gift, sure that its conjunction with her vows was anything but coincidental. As she wrote to Sister Adelgundis: "It reminded me of the way my mother died at the very hour I renewed my vows. Don't take this to mean that I put so much stock in the power of my prayers, or worse still, in my own merits. It's only that I'm convinced that whenever God calls someone, it's not for the sake of that person alone, and that, every time he does call anyone, he's lavish in offering proofs of his love."[40]

---

[40] Stein, *Briefe II,* Letter 262, pp. 104–5.

Chapter 13

Edith Stein's Philosophy: The Nature and Structure of the Person

Edith Stein's colleagues remember how deeply committed she remained to philosophy during her years in Carmel. But after the war, as Germany struggled to come to grips with the horrors of National Socialism, her significance as a philosopher was largely overshadowed by her radical Christianity and voluntary martyrdom. Erich Przywara reflected on this state of affairs in an article written ten years after her death:

> Strangely enough, though the agnostic disciples of Husserl never lost their admiration for Edith Stein, she remained fundamentally unknown among those who had become "her own". She did have a following of sorts—particularly within the Association of German Catholic University Graduates and the Catholic Women's Union—and on the day of her Clothing, an uninterrupted stream of prominent well-wishers passed by the convent grille to offer their congratulations. But as far as becoming a figure in the consciousness of German Catholics, that was only after her deportation and death, and even then, not so much as a thinker or writer, but, understandably, as a symbol of Catholic solidarity with the Jews who had been murdered in the Nazi era.[1]

Fourteen years later, this view was echoed in a speech given by Professor Josef Möller at the dedication of the Edith Stein

---

[1] Erich Przywara, S.J., "Edith Stein", *In Und Gegen* (Nuremberg: Verlag Glock und Lutz, 1955), pp. 65–66.

Student Residence in Tübingen. Having praised her brilliance as a scholar, Professor Möller asked,

> Is there anything else? Yes, there is a great deal. There is the human being who, while never abandoning serious reflection as a Christian, came to place the love of the Crucified above all philosophical investigation and debate. Though to some extent she expressed this love in words (for the words are undeniably there), so fully did she express it in action that, by comparison, the significance of her work seems to become almost insignificant.[2]

Recently, however, the picture has started to shift. Just as each generation has its own understanding of Luther or Saint Thomas, a new generation of scholars has been uncovering a different interpretation of the life and work of Edith Stein. Thanks to a renewed interest in her philosophy on the part of such thinkers as Roman Ingarden, Alois Dempf, and Jan Nota, and the rediscovery of her contribution to the philosophy of education, a more holistic view is now emerging, compared with former tendencies to see her importance almost exclusively in terms of her death.

An early example of this comprehensive perspective was offered by the Benedictine neoscholastic philosopher Father Daniel Feuling of Beuron:

> To me, what most distinguished Edith Stein was the breadth of her intellectual vision and a corresponding emotional vitality and sensitivity. She had a yearning to attain to the deeper sense of man's being and existence that kept her constantly on the watch, both personally and as a scholar, for the great interconnections which permeate existence—in man, in the world, and in being itself. This concern was the fundamental influence on her own thinking and feeling as well as her guiding principle as a teacher and lecturer to Catholic audiences on subjects of human, feminist, and religious importance. More than anything

---

[2] Josef Möller, *Edith Stein—Persönlichkeit und Vermächtnis*, ed. A. Hufnagel (Stuttgart, 1967), p. 15.

else, it was the extraordinary combination of a clear, penetrating intellect and a vigorous, dynamic emotional life that made for her success with her older students and her educated female audience. It was also what allowed her to penetrate to a deeper level of truth in religious issues.

Basic to this predisposition was a strongly rooted philosophical impulse. Philosophy, after all, as the search into truth, being, and existence, is nothing else but these profound interconnections, revealing themselves in refined and expanded concepts to whoever attempts to comprehend, with logical consistency, the essence and activity of every entity he encounters. This philosophical dedication which by adolescence had become second nature to Edith Stein led to the formal study of philosophy under Edmund Husserl, the founder of phenomenology. Like Koyré and Martin Heidegger, she served Husserl as a graduate assistant, maintaining her friendly relations with him up to the time of her entry into Carmel, and even beyond that, to the time of his death.

Edith Stein's fidelity to the philosophical formation she had received lasted her entire life. One of the major fruits of this continued involvement was the translation she made of Saint Thomas' *Quaestiones Disputatae de Veritate,* one of Aquinas' most significant works. Her purpose in undertaking such a demanding task (at which she so brilliantly succeeded) was to immerse herself in Aquinas' conceptual universe and thereby attain to a more genuine confrontation with some of the major philosophical currents of the past. This work, along with her great familiarity with the thinking of Husserl and the other exponents of the phenomenological method, won her such esteem, even beyond the German-speaking countries, that she was invited by the directors of the Societé Thomiste to participate in the conference of hand-picked philosophers and scholars to be held at Juvisy in September 1932. There, following the initial two lectures given at the Journée d'Etudes. Dr. Edith Stein played a very prominent part in the ensuing discussion, distinguishing herself from the other German participants both by her fluency in French and by her ability to express her ideas with complete freedom, restricted though she was to the material of the foregoing lectures and the preceding dialogue. Her frequent contributions gained her the enthusiastic approval of a group composed, for the most part, of extremely prominent male scholars.

Once she had entered the Cologne Carmel, she deeply appreciated the foresight her superiors showed in allowing her to continue with philosophical research within the bounds of her vocation. She continued to function as a philosopher even within Carmel.[3]

Edith Stein's first significant piece of scholarly research was her 1916 doctoral dissertation on the problem of empathy. Years later, in her autobiography, she offered a precis of this early work:

> In the first section, basing myself on a number of indications Husserl had given in his lectures, I examined empathy as a particular form of the act of knowing. Thereupon, I proceeded to a subject of great personal interest which would occupy me in all subsequent writings: the structure of the human person. Even within the context of this early work, it was necessary to take up this theme as a means of clarifying the distinction between the act of comprehending intellectual interconnections and the simple awareness of psychic states. Of prime importance to me in investigating such questions were the lectures and writings of Max Scheler and the works of Wilhelm Dilthey. Once I had finished treating the extensive literature on the subject, I went on to add a few chapters on empathy in its social, ethical, and aesthetic dimensions.[4]

This question of man's nature and the meaning of the human person, which, as a disciple of Dilthey, she was bound to consider, continued to absorb her throughout her career. It emerged next in a lengthy phenomenological study she described as her *Habilitationsschrift* in a 1920 letter to her friend

[3] Daniel Feuling, O.S.B., "Edith Stein", in *Edith Stein: Die Frau in Ehe und Beruf. Bildungsfragen heute* (Freiburg: Herderbücherei, 1963), Bd. 129, pp. 162–63.

[4] Edith Stein, *Aus dem Leben einer jüdischen Familie. Kindheit und Jugend*, Edith Steins Werke, Bd. VII (Louvain: Nauwelaerts/Freiburg: Herder, 1965), p. 279.

Fritz Kaufmann. The work, *Toward Establishing a Philosophical Basis for Psychology and the Cultural Sciences,* was composed of three parts: "Psychic Causality", "The Individual and the Community", and "An Examination of the State". Of the two themes treated in her doctoral dissertation, empathy and the structure of the entity that she called "the psychological individual", it was the latter she returned to here. "The deepest, most provocative, and also most highly questionable considerations in 'The Individual and the Community' [wrote Roman Ingarden] are those dealing with the structure of the human person—the soul . . . the spirit."[5]

Similarly, it was the issue of man's essence and structure that figured predominantly in both her 1931 Münster lectures and in the investigations that made up her magnum opus, *Finite and Eternal Being.* Whether or not, as has been claimed, her ontology lacks originality, it ought to be emphasized that it is the question of man's psycho-physical structure that occupies the central position. "This", says Ingarden, "is what stimulates her thinking, what she truly wishes to find out about."[6]

Given such a trend, Ingarden has felt obliged to ask why Edith Stein did not proceed immediately to the investigation of the person rather than beginning with the notion of empathy. He offers a number of possible arguments: "First of all, she had a very strong interest in foundational research, in establishing a philosophical basis for the cultural sciences. Secondly, she looked to empathy to clarify the theoretical foundations of knowing not only within the individual but within human society as a whole."[7]

Based on close professional association with Edith Stein, Ingarden has suggested more personal motivations for her attraction to the question of empathy:

[5] Roman Ingarden, "Über die philosophischen Forschungen Edith Steins", in *Freiburger Zeitschrift für Philosophie und Theologie,* 26 Jg. (Fribourg, 1979), p. 471.
[6] Ibid., p. 473.
[7] Ibid.

What interested her most was the question of defining the possibility of mutual communication between human beings, in other words, the possibility of establishing community. This was more than a theoretical concern for her; belonging to a community was a personal necessity, something that vitally affected her identity.

At Göttingen, as I've already mentioned, a community of this type existed among the philosophers. People could tell what others were thinking without anyone having to say a word; even after a break of several years, all it took was a couple of words and you knew right away what someone was working on. Edith Stein put down deep roots into this community. For years afterward, as far as she was able, she kept in touch with the other members of the group.

It's also clear, as I learned from her recollections, that she needed to belong to a national community—to think of herself as a member of a particular country. I still remember how she went through the entire war with the attitude of someone always on the verge of beginning a one-man battle. She was determined to serve; there was no question about it. During the time she worked as Husserl's graduate assistant, she wrote me letter after letter asking whether she had the right to waste her time on philosophy and other such nonsense when there were people out there dying whom she should be helping.

Thus, we can see that it was essential to her personally that a community of this sort should exist and that what she was doing was examining the theoretical foundations necessary for such a community. Later on, in "The Individual and the Community", she considered the various ways that relationships can be established between individuals, and here again empathy appears precisely as one of these possibilities. All these issues were very closely interrelated in her thinking.[8]

Translating the *Quaestiones Disputatae de Veritate* led to a change of focus on the part of the phenomenologist. Convinced from her study of Saint Thomas that Christians could licitly engage in philosophical reflection, she determined to attempt an integration of her newly discovered scholastic in-

[8] Ibid., p. 472–73.

sights with her prior phenomenological training. Her suit-
ability for this task has been attested to by the philosopher
Alois Dempf, who recognized in Edith Stein an unusual "capacity for listening and expression", coupled with a special degree of receptivity to the teaching of the older masters. *Finite
and Eternal Being,* the work she revised and completed in Carmel, was the major fruit of her efforts in this direction. In it,
she sought to unite the Thomistic approach to knowing with
the contemporary inquiry into man's personal being.

Dempf has paid tribute to the value of this synthesis:

> *Finite and Eternal Being,* Edith Stein's magnum opus, may be re-
> garded as a presentation in reverse order of the central philo-
> sophical treatise of Aquinas, the *Investigations concerning Truth.*
> Whereas Thomas begins with divine wisdom and truth and
> ends with the human act of knowing, in line with the basic
> principle of speculative philosophy *Cognoscere sequitur esse*
> (knowing follows from being)—so that God sees everything
> based on his being God, while man sees everything in a human
> way (*In Deo omnia Deus, in homine omnia humaniter*)—Edith
> Stein, on the other hand, moved by the same concern for be-
> ginners that motivated Thomas in the *Summa,* begins with or-
> dinary human acts of perception. Before doing so, she has
> naturally argued for the necessity of a shift from a phenomeno-
> logical method to an ontological one—from considering enti-
> ties in their manifestations to seeing them in the ground of their
> being, in their essence and their reality. This justification of her
> own transfer from one master to another should, however, not
> be taken as a denial of the legacy she received from Husserl: that
> ability to describe a particular set of circumstances with the ut-
> most exactitude. There are, in fact, certain places where Edith
> Stein's insights have led her to supplement Thomas' position,
> rather than simply support it. In such cases, the additions are al-
> ways put forward with the prudent concern of a person who
> has learned to appreciate the values of the tradition and has no
> intention of abrogating it. The method that she pursues in her
> study is, first, to provide a simple, straightforward presenta-
> tion of the matter at hand; second, to examine its inner meta-
> physical make-up; and finally, taking it as a "reflection", to

derive it from its exemplar in the divine wisdom. From first to last, it is an approach that is true to reality, a consistent critical realism. . . .

Edith Stein was right to make personal being, through which man most clearly reflects the Creator, the basis of her attempt to comprehend the reflective nature of all created reality. Moving beyond Thomas in her treatment of person and spirit, she identifies personal being itself, the uniquely existent rational soul, as the genuine principle of individuation, determinative of the person's corporeal aspect as well. She thereby made a not unsubstantial clarification concerning the pure spirits by pinpointing personal being as the bearer of their essence. But much more important, she succeeded in substituting for Augustine's doctrine of the reflection of the Trinity in the three spiritual faculties a metaphysical analogy between the Trinity and all created being.[9]

Back in her early days as a phenomenologist, Edith Stein had learned to approach the world of entities by means of "empathy"—empathy being a form of experience in which the primary emphasis was placed on sense-perception. Contrary to positivism, Husserl had taught her that the thinking person can begin with an experience of objects as they are in their original state. He had denied Hume's position that human perception has already been predetermined by man's ideas and impressions. As Ingarden writes:

> The objects have been given. That is the characteristic mark of this type of experience: that the object gives itself, makes itself present. Husserl employs terms such as "self-givenness", meaning a bodily self-givenness, "self-presence", etc. This he opposes to "representation", which he takes to mean the act of making present to oneself that which is not there—in other words, mere thinking.[10]

[9] Alois Dempf, "Endliches und Ewiges Sein", in *Philosophisches Jahrbuch* (under the editorship of the Görresgesellschaft, 62. Jg. Munich, 1953), pp. 202–3.

[10] Ingarden, "Über die philosophischen", pp. 475–76.

What Husserl wanted was for the thinking person to come to perceive things in their originality, without depending on substitute data. When it came to writing *Finite and Eternal Being,* however, Edith Stein followed another route. Rather than immediately introducing standard phenomenological terms like "empathy" and "experience", she proposed an entirely unrelated system marked by Aristotelian metaphysical concepts like "act and potency". Similarly, in the ensuing discussion on certain points in Thomistic philosophy, it is clear that, despite her defense of phenomenological viewpoints and her careful critique of Saint Thomas, there are many instances where she simply incorporated traditional theological arguments without question. Ingarden has seen in this change "a tragic finale on the part of the author", by which he specifically refers to her abandonment of the Husserlian method in its strict objectivity. No longer adhering to the chief phenomenological principle, "Nothing may be accepted in philosophy for which absolute evidence cannot be produced based on a foregoing analytical procedure",[11] Edith Stein began to appropriate traditional Catholic positions without prior evaluation. Ingarden is not unappreciative of the dilemma Edith Stein was brought to in her intellectual development. From one point of view, he admits, it can be said that Edith Stein had come to the end of philosophy; hence, her attraction to the mystical theology of Saint John of the Cross. Yet he insists that her refusal to continue doing philosophy in the sense she had formerly practiced it constituted a kind of tragedy.

Edith Stein was unwillingly caught in the midst of the ontological debate, placed between the representatives of a traditional, clearly metaphysical, ontology and the advocates of a phenomenological ontology which shied away from all metaphysical assertions. Nevertheless, in *Finite and Eternal Being* she succeeded in making a contribution to the study of the problem of God and in unearthing profound insights on the

[11] Ibid., p. 468.

structure of the human person. She turned again to this latter theme in her final works, struggling, though still with only partial success, to discover a single unifying concept for body-mind-soul-person. Edith Stein was not alone in investigating such issues as human nature, spirit, freedom, existence, and personal being. In her own generation, Hans Lipps, Max Scheler, and Martin Heidegger focused on the same questions.

As regards her last years, Professor Möller holds that Edith Stein's intense piety made it practically impossible for her to bring any genuine intellectual interest to the problems of theology. She herself, it might be noted, was painfully aware of the restrictions her lack of theological training imposed on her work. Möller has also raised questions about her lasting influence as a philosopher:

> For all her undeniable philosophical brilliance, as far as we are concerned her work has become remote. Philosophy has since moved in other directions. It is true that a confrontation with Husserl's thought has yet to be accomplished, but this is the later Husserl, with whom, for all intents and purposes, Edith Stein was not familiar. For her, as for Hedwig Conrad-Martius, the late Husserl remained basically unknown. Heidegger she more or less rejected, based on an overly one-sided reading of *Being and Time*. The further question regarding the possibility of discovering common ground between the later Husserl and the later Heidegger, in spite of all their differences, was, obviously, something that Edith Stein could not consider. Yet today, it is precisely from that angle that we have to consider the whole issue of a "philosophy of being and essence" — very differently from the way that Edith Stein handled it. Today it is the acknowledgment of the limitations of historicity and language, and the further issues such a recognition raises, that seem to offer the best possibility for creating a link between phenomenological thinking and a philosophy of being. Compared to these, Edith Stein's integration of early phenomenology and Christian platonism necessarily recedes into the background. Even taking into account her thoroughgoing critique of Thomas on many individual points, her works remain

too strongly apologetic of a philosophy of essence to which we ourselves can relate cautiously at best.[12]

Yet a forward-looking element does remain in the thought of Edith Stein, in her search for the coherence of soul, spirit, and person. The soul in particular, which she identified as the absolute depth of the person, that which becomes perceptible only in moments of silent receptivity, would emerge as a central element in all her philosophical investigations in Carmel: in *Ways of Knowing God,* in *The Symbolic Theology of the Areopagite,* and, ultimately, in *The Science of the Cross.*

[12] Möller, *Edith Stein,* p. 14.

Chapter 14

Life with God

For Edith Stein, interior prayer and exterior action were inseparably related. She stressed the connection in a lecture she gave in Ludwigshafen shortly before she entered Carmel, using the mystery of the infant God to present her case: "The parting of the ways occurs right at the Child's manger; even there, he is King of Kings and Lord of Lords. 'Follow me', he commands, and anyone who is not for him is against him. We too are confronted with these words, and the decision they pose between light and darkness."[1]

Rather than being some decorative piece of Christmas sentiment, she argued, the Child in the manger is the solemn beginning of a life that leads the believer through the darkness of faith into the beatific vision. The Christian who gives this Child his unconditional allegiance need never worry about the direction of his journey, since, "With those who love God, all things work for the good" (Rom 8:28). But in abandoning his future to God, the Christian takes on another obligation: to reflect his inner experience of God to the world around him. This task of "reflection" has little to do with talking about God. Human language can never do more than stammer, at best, "about the eternal light which is life and love in God: he dwelling in us and we in him, our share in the beatific vision. Anyone who has that Kingdom within him knows soon

---

[1] Edith Stein "Weihnachtsgeheimnis", in *Wege zur inneren Stille,* collected articles, ed. W. Herbstrith (Frankfurt: Kaffke Verlag, 1978), p. 13.

enough when he hears it mentioned."[2] What true evangelical love for God does require, according to Edith Stein, is a radical transformation of natural attitudes. She explained the necessity for this by contrasting natural love with supernatural:

> Natural love extends only to individuals with whom we feel united by reason of blood, character, or common interest. The rest of the world, as far as we are concerned, is made up of "strangers", "people who don't affect us"—in other words, people who become increasingly hard to tolerate and whom we end up keeping as much at arm's length as possible.
>
> For the Christian there is no such thing as a "stranger". There is only the neighbor—the person who happens to be next to us, the person most in need of our help. Whether he is related to us or not, whether we "like" him or not, doesn't make any difference. Christ's love knows no boundaries, stops at no limits, doesn't turn away from ugliness and filth. It was for sinners he came, not for the righteous.[3]

Because Edith Stein regarded love of neighbor as an essential form of the apostolate, she insisted the Christian move beyond the "charity" that makes affection a handout and achieve a state of solidarity with those in need of support. She described the requirements and results of such a change of attitude:

> Natural love aims at possession, at owning the beloved as completely as possible. But anyone who loves with the love of Christ must win others for God instead of himself, as Christ did when he came to restore lost humanity to the Father. Actually, this is the one sure way to possess someone forever. Whenever we entrust a person to God, we find ourselves united to him; whereas, sooner or later, the lust for conquest usually—no, always—ends in loss.[4]

Edith Stein did not intend her ideal exclusively for religious. Like Teresa of Avila, she meant to challenge Christians in the world. So she wrote:

[2] Ibid., p. 15.
[3] Ibid., p. 16.
[4] Ibid.

There's quite a distance between leading the self-satisfied existence of the "good Catholic" who "does his duty", "reads the
right newspaper", and "votes correctly"—and then does just as
he pleases—and living one's life in the presence of God, with
the simplicity of a child and the humility of the publican. But
I can assure you: once anyone has taken the first step, he won't
want to turn back. . . .

If, up to now, a person has been more or less contented with
himself, the time for that is over. He will do what he can to
change the unpleasant things he finds in himself, but he will
discover quite a bit that can't be called beautiful and yet will be
nearly impossible to change. As a result he will slowly become
small and humble, increasingly patient and tolerant toward the
specks in his brothers' eyes, now that he has so much trouble
with the beam in his own. Eventually, he'll be able to look at
himself in the unblinking light of the divine presence and learn
to entrust himself to the power of the divine mercy.[5]

Shortly before entering the convent, in her 1932 manuscript
for "The Ontic Structure of the Person and Its Epistemological Problematic", Edith Stein summarized the connection between Christian faith and Christian behavior: "Only by
following Christ is it possible to hold on to him."[6]

Once inside Carmel, Edith Stein began to reflect on the relationship between the official liturgical prayer of the Church
and the wordless prayer of the heart. Having established in her
article "The Prayer of the Church" that "Christ is the model
of man at prayer; only from him can his disciples learn how to
speak with the Father", she went on to write, "Jesus was an
observant Jew who participated in the Jewish liturgy and who
by speaking the ancient ritual promises filled them with new
life. It was, in fact, when he took the bread and wine of the

[5] Ibid., pp. 23–24.

[6] Edith Stein, "Die ontische Struktur der Person und ihre erkenntnistheo-
retische Problematik", in *Welt und Person: Beitrag zum christlichen Wahrheitsstreben,* Edith Steins Werke, Bd. VI (Louvain: Nauwelaerts/Freiburg:
Herder, 1962), p. 197.

Jewish Passover and transformed them into his Body and Blood that the Church's life actually began."[7]

Edith Stein emphasized the intimate bond that existed between the Eucharist and Christ's atoning sacrifice. Just as the Old Testament expectation had been fulfilled in the Son of Man, so Christ's sacrifice was made present each day in the Eucharist, the Church's central liturgical action. The many sacrifices of the old dispensation had been replaced by one: Jesus Christ, offered in thanksgiving to the Father through the consecrated gifts of bread and wine. This eucharistic transformation, affecting the whole of creation, evoked a response of unceasing praise from the Christian, who expressed his thanks through the symbols, words, and gestures of the liturgy. Only in conjunction with Christ's sacrificial offering—a conjunction established by Christ himself—could the liturgy receive its full authentic meaning.

Edith Stein then introduced the second aspect of Christ's prayer.

> Yet Jesus did more than merely participate in officially prescribed liturgical worship. Perhaps with even greater frequency the Gospels show him praying alone in the silence of the night, on open hills, or in uninhabited deserts. They speak of him praying for forty days and nights before beginning his public ministry, retreating into mountain solitudes before choosing and commissioning his apostles, preparing himself at Gethsemane for the journey to Golgotha.[8]

Though Edith Stein loved all of the stories of the Christ of the Gospels, she was particularly moved by the accounts that depicted him as the man of solitary prayer. Here she found the perfect expression of her own particular mission. Like her predecessors Teresa of Avila and John of the Cross, she regarded the Christian calling primarily in terms of the individual's

---

[7] Stein, "Das Gebet der Kirche", in *Wege zur inneren Stille,* p. 26.
[8] Ibid., pp. 33–34.

transformation into God, convinced that apart from this process all apostolic activity and preaching were unproductive. "The human soul as the temple of God", she wrote. "What entirely new and broad horizons that opens up to us."[9] Her reflections on Christ at prayer gave new direction to her former anthropological and philosophical research on the relation between soul, self, spirit, and person. She discovered that, "The more recollected the person lives in his innermost soul, the greater the power he radiates outward and the greater the influence he exerts on others."[10] Jesus' high-priestly prayer, ascending to the Father from his inmost being, showed her the human soul's capacity for "opening itself in freedom to receive the outpouring of the Spirit".[11]

To Edith Stein, this high-priestly prayer of Jesus figured as a central moment in Christ's "solitary conversation" with God. Although it had been spoken in public, in the company of his disciples, she considered it as offered by Jesus alone, as a prayer on behalf of his uncomprehending companions and the entire world. It exemplified for her the solitary prayer which was the indispensable preparation for the visible events of the Church's history:

> In the silence of the Trinity's inner life, the plan of our redemption was formed. In the concealment of Nazareth, the power of the Holy Spirit came down upon the Virgin in her solitary prayer. Gathered around the Virgin in her solitary prayer, the Church awaited the outpouring of the Holy Spirit. Saul in his solitary prayer during the night of blindness God had cast over his eyes received the answer to the question, "Lord, what would you have me do?" Peter in solitary prayer was made ready for the gentile mission. So it has remained through all the centuries.[12]

[9] Ibid., p. 33.
[10] Edith Stein, *Endliches und Ewiges Sein. Versuch eines Aufstiegs zum Sinn des Seins,* Edith Steins Werke, Bd. II (Louvain, Nauwelaerts/Freiburg: Herder, 1962), p. 405.
[11] Ibid., p. 409.
[12] Stein, "Das Gebet der Kirche", p. 36.

Edith Stein laid particular stress on the contribution great women of prayer such as Bridget of Sweden and Catherine of Siena had made to the Church in critical times. She saw in their life of prayer the foundation of their apostolic fruitfulness. Where, she asked, using the example of her namesake, did Saint Teresa,

> who did nothing for decades but pray in a convent cell, ever get her burning desire to defend the Church's cause or her profound insights into the problems and challenges of her time? Precisely by leading a life of prayer, by allowing herself to be drawn more and more deeply into the "interior castle" until she reached the hidden chamber where the Lord could speak to her. . . . Once this had happened, it was impossible not to "Be aflame with zeal for the Lord God of Hosts". . . .[13] The mystical current flowing down the centuries is not a divergent stream that has somehow been separated from the Church's life of prayer. On the contrary, it is its innermost life. Without it, there would be neither liturgy nor Church.[14]

As to the question of mysticism itself, Edith Stein believed that it was wrong to think of it as an esoteric phenomenon. Rather,

> the mystic is simply a person who has an experiential knowledge of the teaching of the Church: that God dwells in the soul. Anyone who feels inspired by this dogma to search for God will end up taking the same route the mystic is led along: he will retreat from the realm of the senses, the images of the memory and the natural functioning of the intellect, and will withdraw into the barren solitude of the inner self, to dwell in the darkness of faith through a simple loving glance of the spirit at God, who is present although concealed. There he will remain in profound peace, as in "the place of his rest",[15] until the Lord decides to transform his faith into vision.[16]

[13] Cf. 1 Kings 19:10, the motto of the Carmelite Order. —TRANS.
[14] Ibid., pp. 38–39.
[15] Cf. Ps 131:8.
[16] Stein, *Endliches und Ewiges Sein,* pp. 407–8.

Mysticism thus understood was neither the special prerogative of people with visions nor the reward for services rendered — since Christ intended the gospel for all. But the fact remained, Edith Stein continued, that certain people did have extraordinary religious experiences which made them aware of the trinitarian life of God. Even though these experiences could never transcend the limits of faith, compared to the painful endurance of "naked faith", they seemed an earthly foretaste of the beatific vision of heaven. Most frequently, it was those intended for great works who enjoyed such experiences; but, she noted, God could just as easily bestow them on sinners and unbelievers.

Edith Stein's conclusion in "The Prayer of the Church" was that it would create a false dichotomy to oppose silent interior prayer to the "objective" liturgy of the Church and relegate it to the realm of subjective piety. Silent interior prayer was the breath and power of the Holy Spirit moving within the Church:

> Every true prayer is a prayer of the Church, every true prayer has repercussions within the Church, and every true prayer is, ultimately, prayed by the Church, since it is the Church's indwelling Holy Spirit that prays within each individual "with sighs too deep for words" (Rom 8:26). That is the mark of all true prayer, "for no one can say that Jesus is Lord except in the Holy Spirit" (1 Cor 12:3).
>
> What else could "the prayer of the Church" be except the mutual self-giving of God and the soul? In that full and lasting union, the heart is "lifted up" to the highest degree possible and prayer attains to its final stage. . . .
>
> Those who have reached this level truly are the heart of the Church; they have the high-priestly love of Jesus living within them. "Hidden together with Christ in God",[17] they radiate to other hearts the divine love which fills their own and join with Jesus in working toward the fulfillment of his one great goal: the restoration of all things to unity in God.[18]

[17] Cf. Col 3:3.
[18] Stein, "Das Gebet der Kirche", pp. 40–41.

She ended her argument with a warning: whenever this inward abiding with Christ is absent, all vocal prayer will gradually degenerate into mere lip-service.

Edith Stein recognized the need for sound spiritual direction in the life of prayer. She herself had often provided counsel in the course of her years as teacher and public speaker. Converts in particular had sought out her advice. In Carmel, Edith Stein continued her apostolate of direction. A letter of hers highlights the seriousness with which she approached this responsibility:

> Perhaps my refusal to go along with your wishes will make me seem hard and unyielding. Please try to believe that rather than acting out of coldness or lack of love, I'm merely following my conviction that, if I did otherwise, I would only be doing you harm. All I am is the Lord's instrument; my job is to lead others to him. When I see that this is not happening because interest is focused on me personally, I can't serve as his instrument any longer and have to ask him to help some other way. Fortunately, he's not restricted to one.[19]

Edith Stein was aware of the director's limitations. Apart from constantly redirecting his client's will back to the goal and attempting to remove the obstacles along the path, he remained an observer, since, "Holiness is a form of the soul that has to emerge from the inmost core, from a level inaccessible both to external influences and to the efforts of the will."[20] Yet even though a director might be unable to offer immediate help, in the last resort, "his effectiveness could be considered as comparable to that of the sacraments. Holy souls as vessels

---

[19] Edith Stein, *Selbstbildnis in Briefen* I. Teil 1916–1934, Edith Steins Werke, Bd. VIII (Druten: De Maas und Waler/Freiburg-Basel-Vienna: Herder, 1976), Letter 76, p. 77.

[20] Edith Stein, "Eine Meisterin der Erziehungs- und Bildungsarbeit: Teresia von Jesus", in *Katholische Frauenbildung im deutschen Volk,* 48 Jg., February 1935, p. 129.

of grace have a sanctifying and transforming effect by their contact alone."[21]

In her 1938 article, "Sancta Discretio", Edith Stein described the essential characteristics of a good spiritual director. Along with humility, reserve, and moderation, she included discernment, the traditional Benedictine *discretio perspicua,* treating it as a constitutive element in the gifts of the Holy Spirit. It was this quality in particular, the fruit of long years of personal experience in the spiritual life, that enabled the director to proceed with the requisite objectivity. She outlined its method of operation as follows: " 'Sancta discretio' is radically different from ordinary human acumen. Instead of discerning in the manner of the discursive intellect, through a gradual process of progressive thought, it functions like the eye in broad daylight, effortlessly discerning the objects within its range."[22] To illustrate the spiritual aspect of discernment, she took up Cardinal Newman's comparison between the gentleman and the saint. While both appear identical in ordinary circumstances, Newman had written, at critical moments, when help is urgently needed, the gentleman has nothing to offer but finesse. He cannot see deeply enough into the hearts of those who have confided in him to be of genuine service. The reason for this, Edith Stein explained, is that to the gentleman,

> the thoughts of the heart and the inner recesses of the soul necessarily remain concealed. It is only the Spirit who can penetrate these, even as he penetrates all things, even the depths of God. True supernatural *discretio* will only be found where the Holy Spirit is in command. This means that a soul will have to be entirely devoted and unfailingly responsive to this honored guest, eager to hear his voice and carry out his wishes.[23]

[21] Ibid.
[22] Stein, "Sancta Discretio", in *Wege zur inneren Stille,* p. 53.
[23] Ibid., p. 51.

Edith Stein's own joy in the Spirit intimated itself most clearly in the poems she wrote in Carmel:

> Who are you, kindly light, who fill me now,
> And brighten all the darkness of my heart?
> You guide me forward, like a mother's hand,
> And if you let me go,
> I could not take a single step alone.
> You are the space,
> Embracing all my being, hidden in it.
> Loosened from you, I fall in the abyss
> Of nothingness, from which you draw my life.
> Nearer to me than I myself am,
> And more within me than my inmost self,
> You are outside my grasp, beyond my reach,
> And what name can contain you?
> You, Holy Spirit, you, eternal Love![24]

---

[24] Edith Stein, *Gedichte und Gebete aus dem Nachlass,* 2d ed. W. Herbstrith (Munich: Verlag G. Kaffke, 1981), pp. 23–24.

Chapter 15

Escape to Holland

By the year 1938, the situation in Germany had grown steadily worse. It was clear to anyone with political insight that Hitler had decided on going to war. All that he lacked was "war criminals" who would force Germany to take defensive action. He found what he was looking for in the defenseless Jews. Confronted with this situation, Edith Stein refused to abandon hope. She was convinced that, like Esther pleading before King Ahasuerus, she had a mission to accomplish on her people's behalf. Though its precise nature continued to elude her, she had enough of a sense of it to be able to write to Mother Petra:

> I firmly believe that the Lord has accepted my life as an offering for all. It's important for me to keep Queen Esther in mind and remember how she was separated from her people just so that she could intercede for them before the king. I myself certainly am a poor and insignificant little Esther, but I take comfort from the fact that the King who has chosen me is infinitely kind and merciful.[1]

One way she imagined that her sacrifice might be offered was by having to live outside the enclosure:

> In any case [she wrote], I think it's a safe method to do everything possible to become an empty vessel for divine grace. "Set

[1] Edith Stein, *Selbstbildnis in Briefen* II, Teil 1934–1942, Edith Steins Werke, Bd. XI (Druten: De Maas and Waler/Freiburg-Basel-Vienna: Herder, 1977), Letter 281, p. 121.

*At the Carmel in Cologne just before
her departure for Holland (1938).*

your heart free from everything, seek God, and you will find him" (Teresa of Avila).[2]

Of course it would be hard to live outside the enclosure, apart from the Blessed Sacrament. But God himself dwells within us, the entire Blessed Trinity, and as long as we know how to construct a well-protected interior cell and retreat there as often as we can, we can't lack for anything, anywhere in the world. That's the way the priests and religious who are in prison will have to keep themselves going. For those who understand it properly, it could turn out to be a time of great blessing.[3]

The S.S. attack of November 8 removed any lingering doubts about the true state of affairs. The morning after the attack there was still an odor of death hanging over the streets of Germany. All through the night, Jewish citizens had been mercilessly driven from their homes with billy clubs, and their businesses demolished or confiscated. In a matter of hours, their lives as members of German society had been destroyed. Even the synagogues had been burned. There was no public outcry against the violence; very quickly the Germans had learned that any such protest would be ruthlessly and immediately suppressed. The time had come in Germany when the Aryan felt as unsure of his safety as the Jew.

As news of these events made their way into the convent, Edith Stein listened like "someone numbed with pain".[4] Without condemning the murderers, she was overcome with horror at the abyss of sin and suffering that threatened to swallow both friend and enemy. Characteristically, however, she soon transformed this initial response into an act of voluntary atonement. She expressed this in a letter to Mother Petra that December:

[2] Ibid., Letter 277, p. 116.
[3] Ibid., Letter 278, p. 118.
[4] Teresia Renata Posselt, *Edith Stein. Eine Grosse Frau unseres Jahrhunderts,* 9th ed. (Freiburg-Basel-Vienna: Herder, 1963), p. 211.

One thing I should tell you: when I entered, I had already chosen the religious name I wanted, and I received it exactly as I
had asked for it. "Of the Cross" I saw as referring to the fate of
the people of God, which even then was beginning to reveal itself. As I understood it, anyone who recognized that this was
the Cross of Christ had a responsibility to bear it in the name
of all. I know a little more now than I did then what it means
to be betrothed to the Lord in the sign of the Cross. But it's not
something that can ever be understood. It is a mystery.[5]

Edith Stein's brothers and sisters, roused by the terrible oc-
currences of the *Kristallnacht,* applied to emigrate to America.
This was no easy matter: the German government demanded
overseas sponsorship for each of the would-be emigrants. Else
and Erna Stein and their families were lucky enough to make
the necessary arrangements and sail to America, and Arno
Stein had already settled there, but Paul and Frieda Stein's ap-
plications were turned down. Rosa's future was another issue
to be determined. As for Edith herself, with Palestine barring
the way to further immigration, the prioress decided to have
her transferred to the Dutch convent of Echt.

Leaving Cologne was again a difficult separation. As one
sister reported it,

As the political situation became more and more critical, Edith
Stein decided it would be dangerous for the convent if she remained any longer: the events of November 8, 1938, had made
it essential to act immediately. You could see the sadness that
had taken hold of her; the old familiar cheerfulness was gone.
God knows what she was going through worrying about her
people, her family, and her community—she never told us
anything. She carried it all by herself in silence.

She left the convent on December 31, 1938. It was a painful
separation for everybody. I had come to feel a heartfelt love and
admiration for her and wondered what life would be like without her. On account of the upcoming departure, that last
Christmas together was very subdued. Then it came time for

[5] Stein, *Briefe II,* Letter 287, p. 124.

her to go. We gathered in the recreation room to say goodbye. One by one, she embraced each of the sisters, but by the time she reached me, I couldn't keep back the tears any longer, and all I said was her name. That shook her a little; for a moment she lost her self-control and began to cry with me. But it was only an instant; then, she regained her composure and left.[6]

Edith Stein was driven across the border under cover of darkness on New Year's Eve. Her first letters from Echt show her struggling against her homesickness:

I don't need to tell you how painful I found it parting from my beloved Carmelite family in Lilienthal—especially the older sisters.[7]

Though it was a difficult decision for all of us for me to leave the convent in Cologne, I was firmly convinced that it was God's will and the only way to prevent even worse things from happening. The community here has taken me in with the greatest affection, doing their best to get me the entrance papers as quickly as possible and smoothing the whole transition with their prayers.[8]

Yet Echt did have something of home about it—the sisters from the Cologne community, expelled during the *Kulturkampf,*[9] had founded it in 1875—and Edith Stein found herself making a rapid adjustment. With accustomed generosity, she was soon responding in kind to the thoughtfulness with which the Dutch sisters surrounded her. From this point on her letters radiate an imperturbable peace: "Once again, I feel as if everything is new for me. Everyone here is treating me with so much love. Pray with me that I can find a way to reciprocate

[6] Report of Sr. Teresia Margareta Drügemöller, O.C.D., Edith-Stein-Archiv, Karmel Köln.

[7] Stein, *Briefe II,* Letter 290, p. 127.

[8] Ibid., Letter 293, p. 129.

[9] The *Kulturkampf* was a conflict between the German government under Bismarck and the Catholic Church, resulting in the temporary expulsion of a number of religious orders. — TRANS.

and make myself useful to the community. . . . He who has laid the Cross on my shoulders has managed to make it sweet and light."[10]

Though from the practical standpoint, Edith was no more able to make herself useful in Echt than in Cologne, the sisters came to treasure "their philosopher" for her dedication toward ordinary tasks. She appreciated their understanding. "Already, in such a short time, I've experienced so much kindness that I can't help feeling grateful. It's clearly God's will that has brought me here—and that is the safest haven of peace."[11] As always, her sense of the divine goodness led to an active concern for others in need:

Ever since coming here, I find my predominant feeling has been gratitude: for being allowed to live here, for this being the kind of community it is. That doesn't mean I'm not constantly aware that here we have no lasting dwelling-place. But as long as God's will is accomplished in me, I ask for nothing else. It's up to him how long I stay here and what will happen after that; these are things which I don't need to worry about. What I do have to pray for is the ability to be faithful under all circumstances. As for the people who have heavier burdens than I do, without the benefit of being solidly rooted in the Eternal, anyone who joins me in praying for them has my heartfelt gratitude too.[12]

Written at a time of interior anguish, when she was plagued by anxiety about her family's future, these words of boundless confidence and trust testify to her years of "resting in God". This is what allowed her to console others in the midst of her own desolation and gratefully respond to the smallest kindnesses. Again and again, her final letters return to this central theme: do everything you can to give joy to others; let God

[10] Ibid., Letter 290, p. 127.
[11] Ibid., Letter 294, p. 131.
[12] Ibid., Letter 300, pp. 136–37.

guide you without resistance; fill up the emptiness of your heart with love of God and neighbor.

During that year, Edith Stein composed three acts of self-oblation — for the Jewish people, for the averting of war, and for the sanctification of her Carmelite family. Unwilling to bear the Cross in name alone, she wanted to be genuinely conformed to her crucified Lord. And, as a sister at Echt remarked: "When a person of Edith Stein's caliber offers that kind of sacrifice, God takes up the offer." One of these prayers was submitted to the prioress on Passion Sunday 1939, shortly before the outbreak of the war:

> Dear Reverend Mother:
>
> Please permit me to offer myself to the Heart of Jesus as a sacrifice of atonement for true peace, that if possible the reign of Antichrist might be broken without another world war and a new social order might be established. I would like to do it today, if I could, since it is already the final hour. I know I myself am nothing, but Jesus desires it, and I am sure he is asking it of many others in these days. [13]

Edith Stein's spontaneous desire to join in atonement with the many who were offering themselves to God should remove any question about her motives for coming to Holland. It was not a flight from reality she sought but entrance into the redeeming action of Christ. She hoped to "fill up through her own sufferings what was lacking in the passion of Christ" (Col 1:24), and she believed the time for her holocaust was rapidly approaching.

In 1939 she composed her final testament. This document, more than any other, reveals her conscious acceptance of her particular mission. To quote from its concluding lines:

> I joyfully accept in advance the death God has appointed for me, in perfect submission to his most holy will. May the Lord accept my life and death for the honor and glory of his name,

[13] Ibid., Letter 296, p. 133.

for the needs of his holy Church—especially for the preservation, sanctification, and final perfecting of our holy Order, and in particular for the Carmels of Cologne and Echt—for the Jewish people, that the Lord may be received by his own and his Kingdom come in glory, for the deliverance of Germany and peace throughout the world, and finally, for all my relatives living and dead and all whom God has given me: may none of them be lost. [14]

Having placed these wishes before her superiors, Edith Stein was content to wait, her mind set at peace.

Another text, written in a similar spirit, was the meditation she presented to Sister Ottilia, the prioress:

Once you are joined to the Lord, you become as omnipresent as he is. Instead of offering assistance in one particular place, like the doctor, nurse, or priest, in the power of the Cross you have the ability to be everywhere at once, at every scene of misery. Your compassionate love, drawn from the Redeemer's heart, can take you in all directions, allowing you to sprinkle on every side the Precious Blood that soothes, heals, and redeems.

Do you see the eyes of the Crucified looking at you with a searching gaze? They are asking you a question: Are you, in all seriousness, ready to enter once again into a covenant with the Crucified? What are you going to answer? [15]

Here Edith Stein expressed her own experience of the Carmelite vocation: a life of unbroken compassion with the millions caught up in the horrors of the war and blinded by its hatred. Rather than being repelled by their suffering, she accepted her share in it, supported by the power of the Cross.

The year 1940 brought her the joy of welcoming her sister to Echt. Rosa, after a series of narrow escapes, had come into Holland by way of Belgium. Now at last, two of the Steins were together again, though the rest were still scattered

[14] Edith-Stein-Archiv, Karmel Köln.

[15] Edith Stein, "Ave Crux, Spes Unica", unpublished article, Edith-Stein-Archiv, Karmel Köln.

through Europe and America. Rosa took on the duties of community portress at the convent, proving herself so capable that she quickly gained the confidence of both sisters and townspeople. Yet Edith and Rosa's positions in the house remained unsettled. Edith had been told that, due to the unstable political climate, she could not expect to make a permanent transfer to Echt after her three-year probation. On similar grounds, the convent declined to accept Rosa officially as portress sister. Pained by these decisions, Edith Stein looked to the Cross for solace. She wrote to the prioress:

Dear Mother:

If your Reverence has had a chance to read Father Hirschmann's letter, then you already know his thinking on the subject. I myself would prefer to do nothing more on the question of my stability for the time being. I place the issue entirely in your Reverence's hands and leave it to you if you wish to consult the sisters, Father Provincial, or the bishop before coming to a decision. Right from the beginning I've been convinced that it is only by feeling the weight of the Cross that one ever gains a *scientia crucis*. That is why I have said with all my heart: *Ave crux, spes unica!*[16]

Your Reverence's grateful child, Benedicta.[17]

Just at this time, reports began to arrive of the dissolution of Carmelite convents in Germany and Luxembourg. Edith Stein prepared for the worst. For years she had been confronting the idea of having to live outside the cloister; now it was an imminent possibility. A letter conveys her reaction: "We may have committed ourselves to the enclosure, but that doesn't put God under any obligation to let us stay in the cloister forever. . . . Yes, we have the right to pray we can be spared this experience, but only as long as we sincerely add 'Not my will, but thine, be done'."[18]

[16] This phrase means "Hail Cross, our only hope!"—TRANS.
[17] Stein, *Briefe II,* Letter 330, p. 167.
[18] Posselt, *Edith Stein,* p. 168.

The poems she wrote in 1940 mirror the conflicting emotions of divine consolation and human suffering that she experienced.

> Bless the bent spirits of those whom griefs oppress,
> The bitter loneliness in their hearts' depths,
> The restlessness within man's very being,
> The sorrow, that no other soul can share. [19]

> He struggled in his fear and sweated blood,
> Begging his Father with his ardent prayer.
> He won his victory on Gethsemane's hill;
> The world's salvation was decided there. [20]

Many a morning, the sisters saw her kneeling at the open window of her cell hours before rising time, her arms outstretched, her face turned toward the tabernacle.

In 1940, the Germans occupied Holland. Edith Stein was once again within the reach of the anti-Semitic persecutors. Correspondence with the Carmelites in Cologne became increasingly difficult, since along with the troops had come the Gestapo, the German secret security police. Somehow, despite the enveloping turmoil, Edith Stein stayed firmly anchored in the Eternal, as shown by a letter to one of the sisters in Cologne:

> I'd be more than glad for a chance to discuss all this with you, but I don't think it's simply an accident that we've been deprived of the opportunity. Let us be grateful for what we have: our unity in the Kingdom where limits and boundaries, separations and distances, do not exist.
>
> Ever since a new postulant entered our community, I frequently find myself thinking back to our own first days in the order, reflecting on the wonderful dispensations of Providence that always accompany the journey to Carmel. And yet, I wonder if the stories of souls inside Carmel aren't somehow even

[19] Edith Stein, *Gedichte und Gebete aus dem Nachlass,* 2d ed., ed. W. Herbstrith (Munich: Verlag G. Kaffke, 1981), p. 21.

[20] Ibid., p. 17.

more marvelous. These stories are hidden in the heart of God, and whenever we think we understand them, we're only catching a glimpse of the mystery God has reserved to himself till the day when all is to be revealed. Nothing gives me greater joy than the hope I have in this future vision. It is faith in our hidden stories that ought to console us when what we see externally in ourselves and in others tends to depress us.[21]

Peace in the midst of desolation—this paradox of her final months was well expressed by Charles de Foucauld: "What could be meant by a peace which is not like the kind the world gives? It is a peace . . . stronger than suffering. Not a peace without warfare, but peace despite warfare, within warfare, beyond warfare. It is the peace of a soul that through love has come to dwell entirely in heaven and to share in heaven's own peace, regardless of anything earthly that can happen to it."[22] Edith Stein would not succumb to despair. The sisters remembered her as unfailingly serene and cheerful, careful to avoid imposing her burdens on anyone.

The year the Germans entered Holland, the sisters elected Sister Antonia to be their prioress. Eager to make use of Edith Stein's intellectual abilities, the new superior assigned her to teach the postulants Latin and begin training Rosa in the basics of Carmelite life. She also asked her to write a book on Saint John of the Cross in commemoration of the upcoming quadricentennial in 1942. In order to leave her free for research, Sister Antonia dispensed her from regular housework. The assignment came at an opportune time. Shortly before, Edith Stein had written to a Dominican friend: "Personally, I find it a help when you send me your requests. It's only when somebody puts a question in front of me that I actually think; otherwise my mind is generally unoccupied. It's good for it to get a little stimulation once in a while when it can still be of use to

[21] Stein, *Briefe II,* Letter 320, p. 157.

[22] Michel Carrouges, *Charles de Foucauld. Forscher und Beter* (Freiburg: Herder, 1957), p. 338.

someone."[23] From the start, the project proved a source of deep joy: "I'm just beginning to collect material for a new book. Our dear Mother wants me to return to intellectual work as far as the organization of our life and present circumstances permit, and I'm glad to have the chance to work on something like this again before my brain gets completely rusty."[24]

Asked at this time to read to the sisters to prepare them for their hour of silent meditation, Edith Stein chose John of the Cross' earliest work, *The Ascent of Mount Carmel*. This led her to reflect to Mother Petra: "This was also the book that I meditated on during my Clothing retreat. Ever since then, I've gone up one level each year—in reading the works of our Father, Saint John, not in ascending the mountain. As far as that goes, I'm still at the very bottom."[25] Like Ignatius of Antioch, who shortly before his martyrdom told his congregation, "Now I am beginning to be a Christian",[26] Edith Stein considered herself a beginner right to the end of her life. She set about studying Saint John with the spirit of a humble disciple: "As a result of the work I'm engaged in, I find myself living almost continually in the world of our holy Father Saint John. This is truly a great grace. Do pray, Reverend Mother, that I may produce something worthy of his celebration."[27]

Edith Stein was particularly struck by a drawing of Christ Crucified that John of the Cross had done. So powerfully did it affect her that, in addition to mentioning it in several letters, she copied it to send as a gift:

Here, Reverend Mother, is my attempt to copy out for you the picture our Father Saint John did on a little scrap of paper, about 5 cm. in size, after he had his vision of Christ Crucified

[23] Stein, *Briefe II*, Letter 311, p. 146.

[24] Ibid., Letter 316, p. 153.

[25] Ibid.

[26] Ignatius von Antiochien, *Briefe* (Freiburg: Herder, 1942), p. 35.

[27] Stein, *Briefe II*, Letter 328, p. 165.

in the convent of the Incarnation. The reproduction that I have in Father Bruno's book is not all that clear, and besides, an artist is the last thing I am. But I've copied it out with great reverence and love, with the hope it will give you some idea of the original.[28]

John of the Cross' drawing is a masterful pen and ink study that sharply contrasts the rough, heavy Cross and the delicate body of the Crucified. The torso tilts forward, almost as if not touching the crossbeam; the arms, though supported by thick iron nails, seem to be pulling away from the wood. The knees are bent forward, and the feet press against the vertical beam in an attempt to gain impetus for flight. Stretched to its very limits, the body nonetheless radiates the power of the Resurrection. Christ's face, which leans against his bosom, smiles in a way that transcends suffering—a smile of patience in victory. All in all, the man on the Cross appears to be leaving the Cross behind him. He is more truly hovering than hanging, ready for flight into another world.

[28] Ibid.

Chapter 16

Final Accounts

It had been twenty-five years earlier, at the death of her friend Reinach, that Edith Stein first encountered Christ in the sign of the Cross. She had been sealed with this sign in baptism and had sacrificed a promising philosophical career to it. She had chosen it as her name in religion to witness to her desire to share in the humiliation and suffering of her Jewish brothers and sisters. Now the sign was to become reality.

Though 1941 brought good reports from America—Erna Biberstein and her family had settled into their new situation, the children were doing well in school—the news from Germany was increasingly grim. By the end of the year, Edith Stein's relatives in Breslau had suffered severe compulsory measures. She described them in a letter she wrote shortly after she learned of them: "My brother and sister badly need our prayers. The sister who remained in Breslau has now been relocated in the country, where she is housed in an attic with eleven other women and forced to work in a sewing shop eight hours a day. My elder brother and his wife expect that something similar will be imposed any day now. They sent me the news without any complaint."[1]

By the beginning of 1942, Edith Stein realized that to keep her new community out of danger, she would have to find a way to get out of Holland. National Socialism, determined to

[1] Edith Stein, *Selbstbildnis in Briefen* II. Teil 1934–1942, Edith Steins Werke, Bd. IX (Druten: De Maas und Waler/Freiburg-Basel-Vienna: Herder, 1977), Letter 328, p. 166.

bring about the complete extermination of the Jews, was extending S.S. operations to all the occupied countries, like a vast network of death. Huge amounts of manpower had been set aside to arrest Jews and register them into work camps where they could be detained and made useful until the time came to deport them to the East. There their lives, "non-Aryan and unworthy of survival", would be terminated. So cleverly did the Nazi bureaucracy camouflage the procedures that many Jews had no idea of what awaited them.

As the crematoria and gas chambers rose in the East, Edith and Rosa Stein, along with thousands of other Jews in Holland, began receiving regular citations from the S.S. in Maastricht and the Council for Jewish Affairs in Amsterdam. During these interrogations, which often lasted for hours, Jews were forced to stand at a three-meter distance from S.S. officials. They were also informed that they would have to wear the yellow star. Though the Dutch Christians responded to these indignities by treating the Jews with emphatic respect, many of them putting on the star themselves to demonstrate their sympathy, the arrests continued unchecked. Edith Stein applied for a Swiss visa. She hoped that by transferring to the Carmel of Le Paquier it would be possible to leave Holland legally. But because of limited living space, Le Paquier informed the Echt community that, while they would be glad to receive Edith Stein, other accommodations would have to be found for Rosa. This was unacceptable to Edith Stein. Although, humanly speaking, Le Paquier was offering salvation, she refused to go to Switzerland without her sister. She continued to write and wait in faith. As she wrote to Cologne in June: "For months, I've been carrying a scrap of paper with the words of Matthew 10:23[2] pinned over my heart. As far as Le Paquier is concerned, the negotiations are still going on, but I've been so

---

[2] This verse reads: "When you are persecuted in one town, take refuge in another." — TRANS.

absorbed in our Father John that everything else seems indifferent to me."[3] Determined to finish *The Science of the Cross,* she used every available moment for research, often working to the point of exhaustion.

In July, as the number of deportations increased, the situation grew even more urgent. Yet negotiations with Le Paquier dragged on, the Swiss apparently oblivious to the seriousness of the danger. Hoping to bring the sisters to safety, the Carmelites in Cologne did what they could to support the efforts of the Echt community.

Meanwhile, throughout Holland, resistance to the deportations was mounting. Catholic and Protestant churchleaders, unwilling to remain silent any longer, agreed to send a joint telegram to Reichskommisar Seyss-Inquart.

> The undersigned Dutch Churches, profoundly disturbed by the measures already taken against the Jews of the Netherlands by which they have become excluded from the ordinary life of the nation, have now learned with horror of the proposed action which would evacuate men, women, children, and entire families into German territory. The suffering this would cause to thousands of people, the awareness that these measures are contrary to the deepest convictions of the Dutch people, and, above all, the resistance that such a step would constitute to God's commands of justice and mercy, compel us to petition you urgently not to have this directive carried out. In the case of Christians of Jewish descent, we are moved by a further consideration: namely, such measures would sever them from participation in the life of the Church.[4]

German authorities, in an apparently conciliatory mood, promised that "Jewish Christians" would be left unmolested.

[3] Teresia Renata Posselt, *Edith Stein. Eine Grosse Frau unseres Jahrhunderts,* 9th ed. (Freiburg-Basel-Vienna: Herder, 1963), p. 178.

[4] "Telegramm der niederländischen Kirchengemeinden an Reichskommisar Seyss-Inquart", 1942, in Jakob Schlaffke, *Edith Stein. Dokumente zu ihrem Leben und Sterben* (Cologne, 1980), p. 33.

The bishop informed Edith Stein's community of this development as soon as he learned of it, and every one at Echt breathed easier.

It was a short-lived respite. As the deportation of the majority of Jews continued, the Churches decided to express their concern publicly. They composed a joint pastoral letter for their congregations that included the text of their telegram to the Reichskommisar. Seyss-Inquart heard of their intention at the last moment and vetoed it. While some of the denominations bowed to the command, the Bishop of Utrecht informed the Occupation that it had no right to intervene in ecclesiastical affairs. By his authority, the following pastoral letter, telegram included, was read in all the Catholic parishes of Holland on July 26, 1942:

> Dear Brethren:
>
> When Jesus drew near to Jerusalem and saw the city before him, he wept over it and said, "O, if even today you understood the things that make for peace! But now they are concealed from your sight." . . . Dear brethren, let us begin by examining ourselves in a spirit of profound humility and sorrow. Are we not partly to blame for the calamities which we are suffering? Have we always sought first for God's Kingdom and his righteousness? Have we always fulfilled the demands of justice and charity toward our fellowmen? . . . When we examine ourselves, we are forced to admit that all of us have failed. . . . Let us beseech God . . . to bring about swiftly a just peace in the world and to strengthen the people of Israel so sorely tested in these days, leading them to true redemption in Christ Jesus.[5]

These direct, hard-hitting words were the concrete expression of the bishops' pastoral concern. Undeterred by the threat of danger, they witnessed to the demands of the gospel in an atmosphere of hatred and intimidation.

[5] "Hirtenbrief der niederländischen Bischöfe vom 20. Juli 1942" (cf. Posselt, *Edith Stein*, pp. 181–82).

While the Dutch waited for the enemy to retaliate, Edith and Rosa Stein received news that Paul and Frieda Stein, along with their families, had been deported to Theresienstadt. The two sisters prepared to meet the same fate at any moment.

One week after the bishops' protest, the dreaded vengeance came. On August 2, in a single sweeping operation, all Jewish Catholics were put under arrest, including the members of Catholic religious orders. Since Nazi officials did not dare to move against the Catholic hierarchy directly, they vented their fury on the Jewish Catholics, dragging them into the march to the East in atonement for the Church's defiance.

Up to the very day of the arrests, no one at Echt had any idea of what was to happen. The last few days had passed without incident; the bishop had contacted the community again to assure them that there was nothing to fear. On July 29 Edith Stein had written to the sisters in Germany: "It's still up in the air whether we will be given permission to emigrate; it looks like the process could still go on for quite some time. I really wouldn't mind if the permission didn't come. Having to leave a beloved religious community for a second time would be no small sacrifice. But let it be as God wills."[6]

That year, August 2 fell on Sunday. Edith Stein spent the day in her usual manner, praying and working on the unfinished manuscript on John of the Cross. During the afternoon, she revised the section dealing with the saint's death: "The saint had passed away unnoticed, while Brother Diego held him in his arms. Suddenly, he observed a kind of radiance around the bed. . . . 'Our father has gone to heaven in this light', he said to those present. As he laid out the body along with Father Francis and Brother Matthew, a sweet fragrance was perceived emanating from it."[7]

[6] Stein, *Briefe II,* Letter 339, p. 175.

[7] Edith Stein, *Kreuzeswissenschaft. Eine Studie über Joannes a Cruce,* Edith Steins Werke, Bd. I, 2d ed. (Louvain: Nauwelaerts/Freiburg: Herder, 1954), p. 279.

It was five in the afternoon when the prioress was summoned to the parlor where two S.S. officers waited to question her about Edith Stein. Assuming they had come to discuss the emigration, Sister Antonia sent Edith Stein to speak to them. The officers immediately ordered her away from the grille, giving her five minutes to pack her things. This threw the convent into a state of confusion. Sister Antonia, realizing her mistake, attempted to negotiate with the S.S. men, but without success. The other sisters hastily gathered a few necessary items for Edith Stein, who appeared momentarily dazed. Quickly recovering, she asked the sisters for their prayers and told them to renew their appeal to the Swiss Consulate.

By the time she reached the convent gate, Rosa was already waiting. The two sisters sorrowfully said farewell to the rest of the community. Meanwhile, the street had filled with local residents incensed over the latest act of violence. Surrounded by the crowd and unable to absorb the situation fully, Rosa began to grow disoriented. Seeing this, a neighbor recalled, Edith Stein took her by the hand and said reassuringly, "Come, Rosa. We're going for our people."[8] Edith Stein understood that the last stage of her journey had begun. Together with Rosa she walked to the corner and got into a waiting squad car. In a few minutes, Echt had been left behind.

The eyewitness accounts of several camp survivors make it possible to reconstruct the last days of the condemned. From Echt, the sisters were driven at top speed to local police headquarters at Roermond and then taken to the central camp at Amersfoort, which they reached sometime in the middle of the night. It was there that the Nazis abandoned all pretense of courtesy: the prisoners were shoved into their sleeping quarters with the aid of fists and clubs. At Amersfoort, the retaliatory nature of the arrests became apparent. Protestant Jews and those of partial Jewish descent were quickly released, but

---

[8] *Kölner Selig-und Heiligsprechungsprozess der Dienerin Gottes Sr. Teresia Benedicta a Cruce — Edith Stein,* eds. Teresia Renata Posselt, O.C.D., and Teresia Margareta Drügemöller, OCD, (Cologne, 1962), p. 92.

the Catholic Jews remained under arrest, together with approximately a thousand other Jewish prisoners.

The next day, August 3, was a long drawn-out agony for the prisoners. A mood of extreme depression prevailed among them, the women in particular. One of the survivors, Dr. Lenig, has testified to Edith Stein's efforts to care for the women's needs.[9] His account has been confirmed by another survivor, Peter Loeser, who was able to recognize Edith Stein on the basis of a family resemblance. Loeser wrote:

> What I still recall very clearly is the unworried, or perhaps even cheerful, way that she and the other brothers and sisters accepted the situation. There was no way to tell that a few hours before the police had caught them completely unaware. They even took care of some of the children. This was so different from the attitude of the other prisoners, who seemed paralyzed with fear—and with good reason.[10]

Loeser's testimony refers to the fifteen members of religious communities who were imprisoned at Amersfoort along with three hundred other Catholic Jews. Five of the fifteen—two priests, a lay brother, and two nuns—belonged to the Loeb family, all of them members of the Trappist order. Two friends of Edith Stein, likewise German refugees, were also there: Dr. Ruth Kantorowicz, who had been staying with the Ursulines in Venlo, and Alice Reiz, who had worked in Almelo with the Good Shepherd Sisters. Despite the circumstances of the reunion, the women were grateful to be together. During that day at Amersfoort, the religious gathered regularly to pray the Divine Office and recite the Rosary, spontaneously grouping around Edith Stein as their center. "The influence she exerted by her tranquil bearing and manner was undeniable",[11] one witness remembered.

That night, twelve hundred Jews were put on a train and carried to an unoccupied stretch of line near Hooghalen. The

[9] Posselt, *Edith Stein,* p. 201.
[10] Edith-Stein-Archiv, Karmel Köln.
[11] Posselt, *Edith Stein,* p. 211.

prisoners had arrived at Westerbork, the central detention camp in the north of Holland, to await the disposition of their fate. A survivor related that immediately on arriving,

> there began one of the most horrible things anyone can experience: the camp registration procedure. Hour after hour, we went from table to table filling out all kinds of useless forms and papers. . . .
>
> Once everyone had been assigned to his barracks, it was discovered that husbands and wives had been intentionally separated with no chance whatever of communicating with each other. You can imagine what these people must have felt. Communication was not restored right up to the time they were evacuated on Friday.[12]

After undergoing such senseless indignities as being photographed with their prison I.D. numbers, the condemned were herded into barracks where even the most basic necessities were wanting. More severe than the physical deprivation was the psychological suffering. Many of the prisoners responded by unrestrainedly weeping or moaning. A report by Frau Bromberg, the mother of a Dominican priest, gives Edith Stein's reaction:

> What distinguished Edith Stein from the rest of the sisters was her silence. Rather than seeming fearful, to me she appeared deeply oppressed. Maybe the best way I can explain it is to say that she carried so much pain that it hurt to see her smile. She hardly ever spoke; but often she would look at her sister Rosa with a sorrow beyond words. As I write, it occurs to me that she probably understood what was awaiting them. She was, after all, the only one who had escaped from Germany as a refugee, and this would have given her a much better idea of the situation than the Loebs had, who were still talking about going to work in the missions. As I say, in my opinion, she was thinking about the suffering that lay ahead. Not her own suffering—she was far too resigned for that—but the suffering that was in store for the others. Every time I think of her sitting

[12] Ibid., p. 213.

in the barracks, the same picture comes to mind: a Pietà without the Christ.[13]

As a result of the enforced separation from their husbands, many of the women rapidly sank into a severe depression. Edith Stein did what she could to relieve them. She cared for their hungry, half-abandoned children, washed their clothes and cleaned the living quarters. One of the survivors, Julius Marcan of Cologne, testified:

> It was Edith Stein's complete calm and self-possession that marked her out from the rest of the prisoners. There was a spirit of indescribable misery in the camp; the new prisoners, especially, suffered from extreme anxiety. Edith Stein went among the women like an angel, comforting, helping, and consoling them. Many of the mothers were on the brink of insanity and had sat moaning for days, without giving any thought to their children. Edith Stein immediately set about taking care of these little ones. She washed them, combed their hair, and tried to make sure they were fed and cared for.[14]

Back at Echt, the nuns had spent three anxious days worrying about the fate of the kidnapped sisters. Finally, on August 5, they received a telegram through the Council for Jewish Affairs. An identical message relating to Ruth Kantorowicz had been forwarded to the Ursuline house in Venlo. The telegrams requested warm blankets, medicines, and other basic necessities for the two women. Greatly relieved, the Echt Carmelites competed with each other in finding provisions for the prisoners. Two local men volunteered to drive the trunks to Westerbork.

August 6, the day the men made the journey, was the last day the Jews spent at Westerbork. In the morning they were informed of the impending departure and given permission to write. Edith Stein's final letter, written in a large, firm handwriting on two small pages from an appointment calendar, is

[13] Ibid., p. 214, report of Julius Marcan.
[14] Ibid., p. 192.

a request to the sisters at Echt for warm clothing and toilet articles for Rosa. The note has a matter-of-fact, almost cheerful, tone and closes with the words: "A thousand thanks. Greetings to all. Your Reverence's grateful child. B."[15] To it was attached a final plea addressed to the Swiss Consulate.

Though from the start it had been determined that no one would be released from this transport, a small group of prisoners had received temporary "deferments" that kept them in excruciating suspense. These included Sister Judith, from the convent at Bilthoven, and Edith Stein. Sister Judith's affiliation with the Portuguese Jewish community managed to save her for the time being, but the efforts the Swiss Consulate made on behalf of Edith Stein proved useless. Eventually executed two years later, Sister Judith left a description of how these deferment cases were handled.

> That morning at eleven, I had to present myself to the Commandant again. A number of people sat waiting their turn in a small room. One by one, each of us had to go into an adjoining room to learn the determination of our cases—all of us had deferments. Every time someone returned you could read the decision from his downcast expression. Scenes of the most heartrending kind were enacted there. After a while, a whisper went through the group, like the sound of terror: "All releases have been revoked." I prepared for the worst. . . .
>
> I saw the German Carmelite. Her release had also been cancelled. Pale but composed, she kept on comforting her fellow-sufferers.[16]

For Edith Stein, the time of uncertainty was over. Rather than being sent back to the convent, she was to follow the way of the Cross to the end, in the company of her Jewish brothers and sisters. The men from Echt who, thanks to the kindness of the Dutch police, were able to meet with her when they arrived a few hours later, found her in a relaxed, almost jovial mood. As they said in their statement:

[15] Stein, *Briefe II*, Letter 342, p. 178.
[16] Posselt, *Edith Stein,* p. 210.

After a few very tense moments, the barbed-wire gates opened, and there in the distance we could see Edith Stein dressed in her black and brown habit, together with her sister Rosa. The meeting was both happy and sad. They shook hands with us warmly but could hardly speak at first—so happy were they to see people from Echt. After a little while, the ice was broken, and we handed on the things the Carmelites had sent.[17]

The men recalled how grateful Edith Stein was for all the kindness the Council for Jewish Affairs had shown. One thing that had made her particularly happy was finding priests in the camp who were working with the sisters to comfort the prisoners.

She related all this in a calm and quiet manner. We had both been smoking as she spoke, and after she finished, in the hope of relieving the tension a little, we jokingly offered her a cigarette. That made her laugh. She told us that back in her days as a university student she had done her share of smoking, and dancing too. . . .

For all her quiet composure, there was a lighthearted happiness in the way she spoke to us. The glow of a saintly Carmelite radiated from her eyes. You could feel the heavenly atmosphere that her faith had created around her. Several times she reminded us to tell Reverend Mother not to worry about her and her sister Rosa. . . . In the camp, they had heard that either that night or the one following they would be transported back to their native Silesia to work in the mines. Wherever they were headed, they told us, whatever work they were assigned, prayer would remain their first obligation. She hoped she could offer her suffering for the conversion of atheists, for her fellow Jews, for the Nazi persecutors, and for all who no longer had the love of God in their hearts.[18]

The messengers who had brought supplies from Venlo for Ruth Kantorowicz supplemented this account:

[17] Ibid., p. 188.
[18] Ibid., p. 189.

As the shrill whistle of the S.S. patrol signalled the prisoners back to their barracks, Fräulein Ruth quickly called the Carmelite sister over to introduce us. Her composure and self-control were amazing, given the situation. When I started to express my sympathy, the courageous nun interrupted me and said, "I am prepared for whatever happens." She shook my hand firmly and wished God's blessing for me and my family. I wished her the same, and, in response, she assured me that there was no need to worry about them—they were in God's hands.

When the time came to say goodbye, we could barely get the words out—they got caught in our throats. They all headed back to the barracks together, but when the others turned around to wave goodbye, Edith Stein resolutely continued walking.[19]

Ten years after her death, an article by the Dutch official Wielek published in *De Tijd* confirmed the reports of her resignation and courage:

> The one sister who impressed me immediately, whose warm, glowing smile has never been erased from my memory, despite the disgusting "incidents" I was forced to witness, is the one whom I think the Vatican may one day canonize. From the moment I met her in the camp at Westerbork . . . I knew: here is someone truly great. For a couple of days she lived in that hellhole, walking, talking, and praying . . . like a saint. And she really was one. That is the only fitting way to describe this middle-aged woman who struck everyone as so young, who was so whole and honest and genuine.
>
> During one conversation she told me, "For now, the world consists of opposites. . . . But in the end, none of those contrasts will remain. There will only be the fullness of love. How could it be otherwise?"
>
> When she spoke, it was impossible not to be moved by her humility and conviction. Talking with her was like . . . journeying into another world, where for the moment, Westerbork ceased to exist.

[19] Ibid., p. 191.

At one point she said to me, "I never knew people could actually be like this . . . , and I honestly had no idea of how my sisters and brothers were being made to suffer. . . . I pray for them continually." When I asked her if she thought God was listening to her prayers, she answered, "He is listening to their pleading. I have no doubt of that."

Once it became apparent that in a matter of hours she was going to be transported with the rest of the baptized Jews, I tried to find out whom I should notify. I wanted to know if there was some way I could be of service. Would it help, I asked, if I had a reliable policeman telephone Utrecht? With a smile, she asked me not to do anything. Why should there be an exception made in the case of a particular group? Wasn't it fair that baptism not be allowed to become an advantage? If somebody intervened at this point and took away her chance to share in the fate of her brothers and sisters, *that* would be utter annihilation. But not what was going to happen now.

Then I saw her go off to the train with her sister, praying as she went, and smiling the smile of unbroken resolve that accompanied her to Auschwitz.[20]

In the middle of the night before August 7, the Westerbork prisoners were unexpectedly awakened to listen to the names of those to be deported. Apart from six exceptions, the list included everyone. As morning came, thousands of men, women, and children crossed through the camp in an endless line, escorted by the S.S. commandos who had taken the place of the camp police. Slowly they made their way to the train, the religious in their habits standing out strangely. The few who were being left behind stood and waved farewell.[21]

---

[20] Report of Mr. Wielek in *De Tijd,* 1952.
[21] Posselt, *Edith Stein,* pp. 214–15.

Chapter 17

Epilogue

During the war, attempts to find out what happened to Edith Stein after her deportation from Westerbork met with little success. A report on her arrest and imprisonment appeared in the *Osservatore Romano* in 1947, but the dates it gave proved unreliable. Then, in March of that year, the situation began to change: "Professor Max Budde wrote to inform us that his friend, Dr. Lenig, interned at Amersfoort at the same time [as Edith Stein], had been the only person released from custody. In his case, he had been given help from the outside, due to his prominent position in the resistance against the Third Reich."[1] A letter from Lenig followed in April:

> As far as can be humanly determined, the information on the victims' death notices is correct. It is absolutely certain that the transports that carried the victims travelled by way of Schifferstadt. From other transports, we know of similar cases where these hopeless unfortunates managed to attract the attention of friends and relatives who happened to be at the station. This puts it well within the realm of possibility that someone actually saw, or perhaps even spoke with, the deceased. The officially attested death of her Carmelite sister should also be taken as certain. Without doubt, it has been established that she died in Auschwitz and was not murdered in Holland.[2]

[1] Teresia Renata Posselt, *Edith Stein. Eine Grosse Frau unseres Jahrhunderts,* 9th ed. (Freiburg-Basel-Vienna: Herder, 1963), p. 200.
[2] Ibid., pp. 200–201.

Lenig's letter referred to an incident contained in the preliminary proceedings for Edith Stein's beatification.[3]

> Our last reliable account of a meeting with Edith Stein comes
> from Valentine Fouquet, then stationmaster in Schifferstadt (in
> the Palatinate). On August 7, 1942, Fouquet was standing on
> the platform when the train from Saarbrucken pulled in with an
> additional sealed compartment carrying prisoners. A woman
> in dark clothing hailed him from inside the compartment and
> asked him whether he knew the family of Dean Schwind.
> When he answered that he and the dean had been classmates
> and that the dean himself had been on the platform just a few
> minutes before, the woman asked him to convey Edith Stein's
> greetings to the dean and his family, and let them know she was
> on her way to the east.[4]

"East", as inquiries with the Dutch Red Cross Information
Service revealed, turned out to be Auschwitz. It was here that
the transport that left Westerbork early in the morning of August 7 came to its final destination. Regarding the actual date
of death, in 1950, when the official Dutch Gazette published
the names of all Jews who had been deported from Holland on
August 7, 1942, the following entry was found:

---

[3] Edith Stein's canonical process was initiated under Cardinal Frings in Cologne in 1962 and the results submitted to Rome in 1972. She has been declared
blessed. —TRANS.

[4] *Kölner Selig- und Heiligsprechungsprozess der Dienerin Gottes Sr. Teresia
Benedicta a Cruce—Edith Stein,* eds. Teresia Renata Posselt, O.C.D., and Teresia Margareta Drügemöller, O.C.D., (Cologne, 1962), p. 23.

Fouquet's statement was substantiated in 1982 by Frau Anna Heckmann,
a teacher who studied under Edith Stein in Münster in the years 1930–1931:
"One of my friends, Ilse Eckrich, also happened to be a friend of the
Schwinds. On August 7, 1942, as she and her friend Marie Berkel got off the
train at Schifferstadt, Fouquet, the stationmaster, came up to them and said,
'The train carrying Edith Stein has just pulled out, heading eastward.' Fouquet
then told them that Edith Stein had asked him to deliver her greetings to the
Schwinds on the Ludwigstrasse." (Report of Anna Heckmann, Archiv,
Edith-Stein-Karmel Tübingen.)

Number 44074: Edith Theresia Hedwig Stein, Echt
Born—October 12, 1891, Breslau
Died—August 9, 1942.

The ninth was assigned as the date of death in accord with judicial testimony that there were no survivors from the transport.

Over the years, additional data about Edith Stein's arrest and deportation has continued to emerge. In 1964 an official report was released by the Bavarian Department of Criminal Justice. To quote from this document:

At the request of the Public Prosecutor's Office in Munich, with authority for dispensing information found under the article AR VI, 206/64:

The Bavarian Department of Criminal Justice wishes to inform you of the findings of its concluding report on the fate of the two Stein sisters:

On July 15, 1942, the headquarters of the "Commanding Officer of Security Police and Public Security Administration in the Occupied Dutch Territory" instituted biweekly deportations of the Jewish population of the Netherlands to Auschwitz and other concentration camps. On July 31, Bene, the Foreign Office's representative to the Reichskommisar for occupied Dutch territory, reported to the Foreign Office in Berlin about the opposition this move had created among the Churches. His report read:

When the different Dutch Churches appealed to the Reichskommisar, his response was he would only permit interventions for the Jewish members of the Churches (and arrange the release of the "Christian Jews" shortly before the time of deportation) on condition that the Churches refrain from further action on behalf of the rest of the Jews. This solution was apparently acceptable to the Protestant Churches, which avoided all special announcements or prayers in their congregations. The Catholic Church, however, publicly addressed the issue of Jewish deportation from the pulpit last Sunday. Evidently, the Reichskommisar's position was not made sufficiently clear to everyone.

Enclosed is the excerpt dealing with last Sunday's events taken from today's confidential report of the Commanding Officer of the Security Police and Public Security Administration to the Reichskommisar. I ask you to keep it strictly confidential.[5]

From the commanding officer's private notebooks, however, we now know that even before Bene's report reached Berlin, the fate of the Catholic Jews was sealed. Several days earlier, on July 30, 1942, Dr. William Harster, "Commanding Officer of Security Police and the Public Security Administration in charge of The Hague", had written in his journals:

Re: The Evacuation of the Baptized Jews. A meeting took place at the Reichskommisar's headquarters on July 27. In attendance:

Reichskommisar S.S. Groupleader Rauter,
Generalkommisar Schmidt,
Generalkommisar Wimmer of Intelligence.
The following orders were given by the Reichskommisar:

1. The Intelligence Agency shall find out as soon as possible which of the Protestant Churches made an announcement from the pulpit about the Reichskommisar's telegram.

2. Since the Catholic bishops have interfered in something that does not concern them, deportation of all Catholic Jews will be speeded up and completed within the coming week. No appeals for clemency shall be considered. On Sunday, August 2, Generalkommisar Schmidt will publicly respond to the bishops' intervention at the Party gathering in Limburg.

3. As per my suggestion, an investigation will be conducted regarding the possible nationalization of some of the larger Catholic charitable institutions. Generalkommisar Schmidt specifically mentioned the Catholic hospitals in Groningen (signed: Harster).[6]

---

[5] Teresia Margareta Drügemöller, O.C.D., *Briefauslese 1917–1942* (Freiburg, 1967), pp. 141ff., and Jakob Schlaffke, *Edith Stein. Dokumente zu ihrem Leben und Sterben* (Cologne, 1980), pp. 9ff.

[6] Ibid., p. 143.

Along with the report of the Department of Criminal Justice, the year 1964 also witnessed the interviews of several concentration camp survivors in connection with the fate of Edith Stein. While the three men—Maurice Schelekes, Josef van Rijk, and Jesaija Veffer—proved unable to furnish direct evidence about her, their reports confirmed the numerous descriptions of the brutality of the Nazi extermination procedures.

Finally, in 1982, an article by Johannes Wieners appeared in the Kölner *Rundschau* in commemoration of the fortieth anniversary of Edith Stein's death. Wieners claims that on August 7, 1942, he spoke with Edith Stein. While there is no way of proving this with certainty after a lapse of forty years, his statement ought at least to be taken as a trustworthy account of the subhuman conditions under which the deportation of innocent people occurred. Wieners wrote:

> I had been working as a mail-truck driver with the Cologne-Deutz postal service. On June 15, 1942, they assigned me to an army post office made up of eighteen men—three out of the eighteen were officers. We were given six weeks of training to turn us into an army post office "for special services" and then shipped off on railroad cars to join the sixth army in Russia.
>
> On August 7, 1942, as our train stood in the railroad yard in Breslau, waiting for the engine to be refueled, a freight train came in on the track alongside ours and halted next to us. When the guard opened one of the sliding doors, we could see people all penned up, listlessly squatting on the floor. There was a horrible stench coming from the car. A woman dressed like a nun appeared at the door, and, I guess because I looked sympathetic to her, she said to me, "It's terrible. We don't even have containers to relieve ourselves." After that, she looked into the distance at Breslau and said, "This is my home; I'll never see it again." I stared at her, wondering what she was talking about. She paused for a minute, then said, "We are going to our death." That really shook me. I remember that I asked her, "Do the other prisoners know about this?" She answered very slowly, "It's better for them not to know."

Some of my comrades saw us together and laughed at me for talking to a Jew. But one of them who had heard what we were saying came over and joined me. The two of us tried to figure out if there was anything we could offer these poor people. But the woman had heard my comrades, and when I asked her, "Can we get you something to eat?" she answered, "No, thank you. We won't take anything."

From the markings on the freight train it was clear that it came from Holland. They hooked up our engine then, and on we went to Poland—but when I got back from internment in 1948, I read about Edith Stein in a magazine. The minute I saw the picture, I knew it was the sister from August 7, 1942. August ninth was the date they had given for her death.[7]

It is very possible that the exact details of Edith Stein's final days will never be fully known. Be that as it may, the way she faced the events of those days has made her into a symbol of the transforming power of atoning love. When her Jesuit friend Father Hirschmann was asked to speak on the theme "Love Transforms Fear, Guilt, and Suffering" at the 1979 *Katholikentag* in Berlin, it was her example that he turned to. He began by recalling the period between her baptism and her entrance into the convent, when

the shadow of anti-Semitic hatred settled over Germany. On the one hand, it was this shadow which barred the way to a university professorship and a full-time scholarly career; on the other, it opened the way to an involvement in the Catholic women's movement, to an apostolate in Catholic education, and, finally, to a vocation in a religious order marked by the love of the Cross.

Inspired by the theology of her great Carmelite predecessor John of the Cross, Edith Stein learned to unite intimately her historically determined cross of membership in the Jewish people with the Cross of Jesus Christ. She became convinced

[7] Johannes Wieners, "Meine begegnung mit Edith Stein", in *Kölnische Rundschau,* August 9, 1982.

that as a Jew she was being called to share in her people's sufferings, and she solemnly committed herself before God not to let her vows or baptism give her the slightest advantage over the most wretched of her persecuted people.

But Edith Stein was not only a Jew lovingly united to the Jewish people; she was also a German united to the German people. And as such, she was constantly faced with the question, "Who will atone for what is happening to the Jewish people in the name of the people of Germany?" It caused her intense suffering that baptized Christians like Hitler and Himmler were taking the guilt of such awful crimes upon themselves. "Who will turn this enormous guilt into a blessing for both peoples?" Ultimately, the answer she came to was that only the victims of hatred could do it, if instead of letting their wounds produce new hatred, they would be willing to carry the suffering of their fellow victims and their tormentors.

I will never forget the conversations I had with this genuinely Christian philosopher when time and time again she would insist that hatred must never be given the last word. Somehow it had to be possible—through prayer and atonement—to obtain the grace of conversion for those who hated. Hadn't Jesus, when he prayed for those who hated him, those who crucified and pierced him, turned his wounds into the symbol of love that proved to be stronger in the end?

There is no question that Auschwitz will always remain for us as a terrifying revelation of the destructive potential of human lovelessness. But there is another revelation at Auschwitz, infinitely transcending the first: that the love which endures the Cross and wounds ultimately overcomes all lovelessness. This is the love that says to the Cross: for the sake of the love which has come to men through Jesus' Cross and wounds, I love you and I testify—hate is not stronger than love.[8]

Forty years after her death, men and women still feel compelled to pay homage to the philosopher and mystic who inspired these words. May her thoughts on the occasion of the

---

[8] Johannes Hirschmann, S.J., "Schwester Teresia Benedicta vom Heiligen Kreuz", in *Monatsschrift des Bundes Neudeutschland,* 34 Jg., 1981, pp. 125–26.

centenary of another great German woman, Saint Elizabeth of Thuringia, help us who honor her memory today to go beyond mere outward commemoration and learn to be molded by her character and spirit:

> Why has our generation become so devoted—I almost said so addicted—to celebrating anniversaries? Is it the weight of the misery we feel that makes us want to escape the gray, oppressive atmosphere as much as possible—to seek refuge in the sun of better days? But flight is an unproductive reason for celebrating: I think we ought to assume there is a deeper, healthier motive behind our attraction to the past. We are a spiritually impoverished generation; we search in all the places the Spirit ever flowed in the hope of finding water. And that is a valid impulse. For if the Spirit is living and never dies, he must still be present wherever he once was active forming human life and the work of human hands. Not in a trail of monuments, however, but in a secret, mysterious life. He is like a small but carefully tended spark, ready to flare, glow, and burst into flame the moment he feels the first enkindling breath.[9]

---

[9] Edith Stein in *Edith Stein: Die Frau in Ehe und Beruf. Bildungsfragen heute* (Freiburg: Herderbücherei, Bd. 129, 1963), p. 106.

Selected Bibliography

Works by Edith Stein in Translation:
Collected Works of Edith Stein. Washington, D.C.:
ICS Publications.
    Vol. 1: *Life in a Jewish Family.* Trans. Josephine Koeppel,
        O.C.D.
    Vol. 2: *Essays on Woman.* Trans. Freda M. Oben, Ph.D.
    Vol. 3: *The Problem of Empathy.* Trans. Waltraut Stein,
        Ph.D.
    Vol. 4: *The Hidden Life.* Trans. Waltraut Stein, Ph.D.
Edith Stein: Selected Writings. Ed. Susanne M. Batzdorff. Spring-
    field: Templegate Publishers, 1990.
The Science of the Cross [Kreuzeswissenschaft]. Translated by Hilda
    Graef. Chicago: Regnery, 1960.
On the Problem of Empathy [Zum Problem der Einfühlung]. Translated
    by Waltraud Stein with a foreword by Erwin Strauss. The
    Hague: M. Nijhoff, 1964.
Ways to Know God [Wege der Gotteserkenntnis]. Translated by
    M. Rudolf Allers in *The Thomist,* July 1946.

Works about Edith Stein:

Baybrooke, Neville. "Edith Stein and Simone Weil". In *Hibbert
    Journal: Quarterly for Religion, Philosophy and Theology,*
    no. 253, pp. 75–80.
——. "The Called and the Chosen: A Comparative Study of
    Edith Stein and Simone Weil". *In Religion and Life,* no. 28
    (1958–59), pp. 98–103.
Collins, James. "Edith Stein". In "The Advance of Phenomenol-
    ogy," *Thought,* vol. 17, no. 67 (1942).
Hanley, Boniface O.F.M. "The Slaughter of an Innocent". In *The
    Antonian* (1979).

---

† This is the English section of the bibliography mentioned in the Foreword. The interested reader should refer to the German original.

Herbstrith, Waltraud. "From Atheism to Sanctity: Edith Stein". In *Carmel*, Journal of the Discalced Carmelites (1976), pp. 8–9.

Oesterreicher, John M. "Edith Stein". In *Walls Are Crumbling: Seven Jewish Philosophers Discover Christ*. New York: Devin-Adair, 1952, pp. 325–72.

Reviews of Individual Works by Edith Stein:

A. *Finite and Eternal Being [Endliches und Ewiges Sein]*

Allers, R. In *The New Scholasticism*, vol. 26 (1952), pp. 480–85; vol. 32 (1958), pp. 132–33.

Kaufmann, F. In *Philosophy and Phenomenological Research*, vol. 12 (1952), pp. 572–77.

Klubertanz, G. P. In *The Modern Schoolman*, vol. 39 (1961), p. 420.

B. *The Science of the Cross [Kreuzeswissenschaft]*

Klubertanz, G. P. In *The Modern Schoolman*, vol. 28 (1951), p. 308.

Sr. Marie Catherine. In *The New Scholasticism*, vol. 37 (1963), pp. 94–97.

Index